Now online at
www.growco.com

THE GROWTH COMPANY GUIDE TO INVESTORS, DEAL STRUCTURES, AND LEGAL STRATEGIES

PRACTICAL ADVICE FOR GROWING COMPANIES AND PRIVATE COMPANY INVESTORS

Clinton Richardson

Amsterdam • Johannesburg • London
San Diego • Sydney • Toronto

Page Compositor: Nicola Ruskin
Cover: Tom Lewis, Inc.

Pfeiffer & Company
8517 Production Avenue
San Diego, CA 92121-2280

ISBN: 0-89384-233-8

Printed in the United States of America.
Printing 1 2 3 4 5 6 7 8 9 10

This book is printed on acid-free, recycled stock that meets or exceeds the minimum GPO and EPA specifications for recycled paper.

DEDICATION

To my entrepreneurial father
F. William Richardson
(1922-1983)

CONTENTS

ACKNOWLEDGMENTS

The *Growth Company Guide* started with a simple idea: that entrepreneurs and investors could benefit from a straightforward source book on raising capital that dealt with how deals are structured as well as how investors are found.

The book's inspiration was my father. His enthusiasm for entrepreneurship and for business help books inspired me to begin this book. He was the quintessential entrepreneur, working long hours making businesses from ideas and loving it. Like most entrepreneurs, he saw life as a challenge to be embraced and enjoyed.

My wife and children also deserve special mention. They sacrificed many family hours and activities while I drafted and redrafted the manuscript. Their enthusiasm and encouragement were as important to completing this book as was my inability to see the folly in expecting a lawyer to write a succinct, "plain English" volume about anything.

The next acknowledgment belongs to Steven Cohen, former special projects editor at *Venture* magazine. His enthusiasm and expertise helped mold this book into the readable version you have in front of you. Thanks, too, to Arthur Lipper III, investor, entrepreneur, and former chairman of *Venture*, for seeing the value in this book and publishing its first version as *The Venture Magazine Complete Guide to Venture Capital*.

Finally, thanks to my partners and associates at Arnall Golden & Gregory, who reviewed portions of the manuscript and offered helpful comments. Thanks also to Robert G. Schwartz, president of Atlanta Cable Sales, Inc., and former director of The Mercer University Center for Innovation and Entrepreneurship, and John J. Huntz, managing director of Noble Ventures International, for their support during the drafting of the book.

INTRODUCTION

The *Growth Company Guide to Investors, Deal Structures, and Legal Strategies* is designed to help entrepreneurs and managers of growing companies improve their odds of raising capital from outside sources. It does so by answering the questions most frequently asked by entrepreneurs and managers of growing companies as they search for funding and, later, negotiate for favorable financing terms.

The Growth Company Guide contains more than 200 entries arranged in alphabetical order. Each entry describes a word or phrase that is commonly used by investors and entrepreneurs to describe an important fund-raising or growth company concept. Together, the entries explain what entrepreneurs need to know to prepare for fund-raising efforts and to attract and deal successfully with investors.

The book is comprehensive. It describes the types of investors who invest in private companies, the methods companies use to attract these investors, and ways to evaluate funding proposals. It includes strategies for negotiating better deals with investors. It also describes methods for protecting company secrets and using stock and other noncash considerations to attract and keep key employees.

The Growth Company Guide is different from other books about raising capital. It is not written by a venture capitalist, who may be biased toward protecting investors, or by an entrepreneur, whose experience may be limited to a few financings. Rather, it is written by an attorney who has more than a decade of practical experience in representing individual investors, venture capitalists, entrepreneurs, and growth companies in company financings, acquisitions, securities offerings, technology, and general corporate matters.

The Growth Company Guide is designed to be a "real-time" source book for busy entrepreneurs and executives. Its A to Z, key-word format helps readers get directly to the information they want. For example, if a reader wants to know how venture capitalists price their investments, he can find out by simply turning to the entry entitled *Pricing*. There he will find a discussion of how investors evaluate and price investments in growing companies. The entry also suggests strategies for negotiating with investors and cross-references the reader to a discussion of the principal alternative pricing method contained in the *Discounted Cash Flow* entry.

If an investor offers funding but wants preferred stock and registration rights, the reader can quickly turn to the entries for those terms and learn the reasons behind the investor's request and the consequences the request may have on the company. In the *Business Plan, Business Plan Format,* and *Summary* entries, the reader will find discussions of how business plans should be written to attract funding with detailed, tested outlines for producing a winning business plan and summary. In each case, the reader will also be directed to other entries in the book that treat related subjects.

The Growth Company Guide's key-word entries address subjects that are vital to a successful fund-raising campaign. The subjects include the venture capital arena and its players, strategies for attracting the right investor, the funding deal and its structuring, company valuations, and technology protection. For the reader's convenience, the entries are not only extensively cross-referenced but organized by subject matter in a complete subject matter index in the back of the book.

Most entrepreneurs have too many things to do and too few resources to do them with to take the time to really learn about raising capital from traditional textbooks. As a result, many good ideas don't get funded. And even the entrepreneur who obtains funding usually finds himself dealing on uneven terms with an investor whose business it is to know the finer points of private company investing.

The Growth Company Guide's format is designed to remedy this situation by helping entrepreneurs become familiar with the language and concepts of venture capital. Its alphabetical design and extensive cross-referencing lets entrepreneurs learn the important concepts quickly and easily while they search for money. In so doing, it improves the reader's chances of raising funds for his company.

Use the book as a tool before and during your fundraising efforts. Don't read it from cover to cover and put it away. Instead, keep it handy and refer to it often. And don't feel that you have to read the book from beginning to end. Start with an entry that interests you and proceed as you like through the others.

Good luck in your search for capital.

A Word of Caution

Do not use this book as your only source of information. It does not answer every question or apply to every situation. Many of the answers in the book reflect personal judgments about what is "standard" or "fair" in the "usual" situation. Those answers may not always apply to your particular situation.

Try to stay current with changes that affect your company, industry, and the capital raising process by reading periodicals and getting good professional advice. Much of what directs the processes of a growth company and the deal structures investors use is related to provisions of the Internal Revenue Code, the securities laws, and methods accountants use to report company operations. These change regularly, as do government programs such as the Small Business Investment Companies (SBIC) program and the Small Business Innovation Research (SBIR) program of the federal government. Presently proposed changes to the SBIC program could increase funds available to growing companies and change the way those funds are invested.

Also, remember that the growth and fund-raising processes differ with each company, each idea, and each investor. They are intense activities that can cloud the judgment of even the shrewdest of businessmen. To protect your interests, get independent counsel and learn as much as possible about the processes.

For simplicity, this book uses the pronouns "he," "his," etc., to represent both genders. Use of the masculine is not meant to slight women or imply that a woman is less likely than a man to be an entrepreneur or investor. It is merely the chosen device to speed the reader through the book without undue focus on any one element of the writing.

A

Adventure Capitalists are entrepreneurs who invest money in other entrepreneurs. Like other venture capital investors, they invest to make money. Unlike traditional venture capital funds, however, adventure capitalists invest their own money instead of money others have placed in their care. Usually, the money they invest is money they made by selling a company they started and made grow.

Adventure capitalists fund new enterprises for a combination of reasons. They know that a wise investment can be very profitable. They believe their experiences as entrepreneurs help them to identify attractive deals. Also, adventure investing gives them something they cannot get from other investments: the chance to relive the excitement they experienced in getting their own businesses started.

For many adventure capitalists, this last reason is the telling motivation. The exhilaration they experienced starting their businesses may be waning. They may operate public companies long past their start-up stages or run divisions of large companies that acquired their businesses. Many have retired from daily management activities. Still, there is something about making a new business succeed that draws them into adventure investing.

Like other investors, adventure capitalists expect to receive and study a business plan before they proceed. They usually require a seat on a company's board of directors and reports from management on the company's progress. Their active participation is important to them. They expect to be consulted by management and to have their advice heeded.

Adventure capitalists do not see as many deals as venture capital firms do. And, while most investigate companies before investing, few do so as thoroughly as a sophisticated venture capital firm would. This, coupled with the fact that they do not have to consult with others before making an investment, often means a faster response on a deal.

The smaller deal flow and the part-time nature of their investment activity mean that entrepreneurs can sometimes get funding from an adventure capitalist when they could not obtain it from a venture capital firm. This is particularly true in smaller financings. Many venture capitalists, with their high administrative costs and large deal flows, will only invest in increments of $500,000 or more.

Adventure capitalists are not so constrained, but their lack of investment experience can cause problems for a company. If the company is delayed in meeting a milestone, the adventure capitalist may feel misled and become difficult to work with—for example, he may refuse to provide follow-on investments he has agreed to make. This may happen even though the company's problems are not severe.

This reluctance to fund subsequent stages can be catastrophic because it forces management to divert its attention to raising money when other aspects of the company's business need managing. And fund-raising can be very difficult with an unwilling investor in a company. His refusal to fund often frightens away other investors. Also, he may have contractual rights that prevent others from investing in the company.

Even binding contracts that require an investor to provide follow-on funding may not be enough to prevent problems. The expense and effort required to enforce those contracts against an unwilling investor may be too great for a company to afford. The result can be an impoverished company forced to begin the search for money anew while dealing with a struggling business and a dissatisfied adventure capitalist.

To protect against this, entrepreneurs should investigate an adventure capitalist's reputation and ability to fund before they accept his money. If he offers to fund the company's needs in stages, management should ascertain how he intends to meet his funding commitments. If he must borrow or liquidate other promising investments to fund the company in later stages, he may become difficult to deal with when the money becomes due even if the company meets or surpasses its benchmarks. *See: Angels, Deal Flow, Due Diligence, Ethics, Venture Capitalists.*

Affirmative Covenants refer to contractual provisions in a venture funding that the company and its management agree to after the funding is complete. These covenants typically appear in the financing or stock purchase agreement and are often accompanied by "negative covenants," which obligate the company to refrain from taking certain actions after the funding. Common affirmative covenants include

- *Access to records.* The company will give the investor and its representatives reasonable access to company records and personnel.
- *Financial reports.* The company will furnish the investor with regular financial reports on the status of the company. Balance sheets, profit and loss statements, and cash flow statements are usually provided monthly, quarterly, and annually. The annual

statements are often required to be audited. Sometimes a short "state of the company" statement is also required from the company president monthly.

- *Budgets.* The company will prepare annual budgets that must be approved by the board of directors or, sometimes, by the investor.

- *Existence and maintenance of property.* The company will preserve its corporate existence and all rights necessary to conduct its business and own its properties. The company will keep its properties in good repair.

- *Insurance.* The company will maintain adequate insurance. Often, the company also agrees to purchase key man insurance on the lives of management.

- *Payment of debts and taxes.* The company will pay its debts and taxes in accordance with normal terms.

- *Compliance with laws and agreements.* The company will comply with all laws applicable to it and perform its obligations under its agreements.

- *Litigation and other notices.* The investor will be promptly notified of any lawsuit, default under a major agreement, or other event which could have a material adverse effect on the company or its operations.

- *Proprietary rights protection.* The company will take reasonable steps to protects its patents, trade secrets, and copyrights. These steps may include securing secrecy or noncompetition agreements from company employees.

- *Use of proceeds.* The company will use the funds provided by the investor in the manner described.

- *Accounting system.* The company will maintain its current accounting system.

- *Board of directors.* Management shareholders will vote their shares to assure the investor of a representative on the company's board of directors.

See: Financing Agreements, Key Man Insurance, Management Agreements, Negative Covenants, Operating Covenants, Reps and Warranties, Take Away Provisions.

Angels are people who provide funding for very young companies to help get them started. The term comes from Broadway, where show backers have traditionally been referred to as "angels." In venture capital, the term refers to an entrepreneur's first investors who put their money in before there is a product or a viable business.

Angels are most often friends, relatives, or business acquaintances who, because of their belief in an entrepreneur's abilities or in the value of his idea, are willing to invest significant sums of money in the entrepreneur long before his business is established. Most invest only a few times during their lifetime and are unsophisticated about investing in small companies. Many invest once, lose their money, and never do it again.

More often than not, angels' investments are poorly documented and not particularly well thought out. Because they lack familiarity with the types of problems young companies face and the difficulty of getting money out of a young company, angels often invest without obtaining an adequate method for cashing out. Entrepreneurs who value the friendship and commitment of their angels, however, will take pains to discuss how angels can get their investments out so that both the entrepreneur and the investors share realistic expectations. *See: Adventure Capitalists, Cashing Out (or In), Seed Capital, Venture Capitalists.*

Antidilution Provisions are agreements that ensure a company's early investors that later investors will not obtain more equity per dollar than they did. Many investors insist on some sort of antidilution protection as a condition to their investing, particularly if they are the company's first major investors. Antidilution protection can appear as provisions of a financing agreement, in the terms of a warrant or option, in a shareholders' agreement, or in any other agreement between investors and a company.

One common antidilution provision provides that the percentage of a company owned by an investor will not be reduced until some future event occurs. The event could be the passage of time, the funding of an additional $500,000, or some other occurrence. Any stock issued by the company before the future event occurs would entitle the protected investor to receive more shares, either for free or for some agreed-upon price.

Another typical antidilution provision requires a company to give an investor "free" stock if it sells stock to a later investor at a lower price. For example, an investor who purchased 100,000 shares for $2 a share would be given more shares at no charge if the company later sold stock to another investor for $1 per share. If the earlier investor receives enough free shares to reduce his average cost per share to the price paid by the new investor (100,000 shares in this example), his antidilution right is called a "ratchet."

Another antidilution provision allows an investor to purchase additional stock if later share prices are lower or if more than a certain number of shares is sold. Preemptive rights and provisions that entitle investors to obtain a percentage of outstanding stock in the future instead of a fixed number of shares are also antidilutive.

There are many other variations of antidilution provisions. Any agreement that tends to insure an investor his relative price advantage or percentage ownership is an antidilution provision.

All antidilution provisions dilute the interests of the shareholders who are not protected by them. This usually includes management. As a result, these provisions should be considered carefully before they are completed. To protect management, all antidilution provisions should stipulate an expiration date. Under no circumstances should antidilution provisions be allowed to survive a public offering of the company's stock or the sale or merger of the company, since they can hamper management's ability to raise funds in the public market or close a favorable merger or sale of the company. Also, whenever possible, investor antidilution rights should exclude the issuance by management of a number of shares for use in an incentive stock option plan or other employee incentive plan to help the company attract and keep key personnel. *See: Dilution (Percentage), Equity Penalties, Financing Agreements, First Refusal Rights, ISOs (Incentive Stock Options), Preemptive Rights, Ratchets, Weighted Average Antidilution.*

Audits are methodical reviews by a disinterested third party of a company's accounts or, more generally, its financial situation. They are usually conducted by independent accounting firms.

Few venture capitalists expect a new company to have audited financial statements. Audits are expensive, and most investors believe a new company's money is better spent in other areas. This is not to say, however, that investors do not expect a company's books to be complete and accurate. They do. Venture capitalists usually examine a company's books and records thoroughly before they invest. Most of them also interview the company's accounting firm and check behind the company's books by calling suppliers and creditors.

When a company anticipates conducting a public offering, it is wise for it to have audits conducted or, at least, to have independent Certified Public Accountants (CPAs) verify the company's yearly inventories. This is because companies are usually required to disclose three years of audited financial statements in their initial public offerings. Sometimes only two years are required for limited offerings and, of course, a company that has been in existence for less than three years can only provide financial statements for the period it has been in business.

The audits required by initial public offerings can sometimes be performed just beforehand, but this can delay the offering and result in unexpected changes to the offering documents when the independent accountants apply their procedures to make the company's statements comply with the requirements of the Securities and Exchange Commission (SEC).

When a company plans to go public, the safer, and often cheaper, course of action is to engage an independent accountant to conduct audits on a regular basis. Most accountants will take this opportunity to get to know the company better and suggest reporting mechanisms that can help management run the company more efficiently. Also, they will prepare statements that comply with the requirements of the SEC so that the company can move more quickly to consummate a public offering. At the same time, they can help management organize other records, such as reports on industry segments, to fit the disclosure requirements of initial public offerings. While audits may seem expensive for a young company, having an independent CPA oversee and review the company's books may reduce the time and cost of having the audit done at a later date. *See: CPAs (Certified Public Accountants), Due Diligence, Going Public, IPOs (Initial Public Offerings), Reports and Records.*

B

Bargain Stock is corporate equity that is acquired at low cost, usually in the early history of a company. Sometimes called "cheap stock" or "founders' stock," bargain stock almost always includes the original stock issued to the company's founders. *See: Cheap Stock, Sweat Equity.*

BDCs (Business Development Corporations) are companies organized under special state statutes for the purpose of providing funds to small businesses in their states. Most can provide debt and equity financing.

BDCs borrow the money they provide to businesses. Because of this, they tend to finance companies in ways that will generate enough cash to permit the BDCs to make their interest and principal payments to their lenders. In other words, BDCs usually lend money instead of making pure equity investments. This way, the companies in its portfolio support the BDC's obligation to repay its lenders by making regular payments of principal and interest to the BDC. Even when a BDC acquires stock in a company, it is usually through a warrant or option to purchase stock that accompanies a loan.

Because BDCs need to make regular debt service payments to their lenders, they (unlike other venture investors) tend to be more interested in a company's ability to support and repay debt in the short term than in the company's prospects for rapid, profitable growth. As a result, BDCs are often precluded from investing in early stage companies or companies that lack the ability to show a profit in the near term. *See: CDCs (Community Development Corporations), Debt Service, SBICs (Small Business Investment Companies), Venture Capitalists.*

Beads and Trinkets is negotiating jargon. It refers to a small concession made by one party in return for a Manhattan-sized concession from the other party.

While conceding "beads and trinkets" in the heat of negotiations may seem insignificant at the time, the negotiator should ask himself why the other party seeks the concession. What seems like a trinket to one party may be quite valuable to the other.

Benchmarks are performance goals against which a company's success is measured. Often, they are used by investors to help determine whether a company will receive additional funding or whether management will receive extra stock. Sometimes management will agree to issue more stock to its investors if the company does not meet its benchmarks, thus compensating the investor for the delay of his return.

Whatever purpose benchmarks serve in a financing arrangement, failure to arrive at one on schedule almost always punishes management in some way. As a result, management should be certain to negotiate conservative benchmarks. Whenever possible, they should be at a level that management, as well as the investors, thinks is achievable realistically. In that way, failure to achieve the benchmark is a true signal that something is wrong with the company or its plans.

For example, a benchmark could be stated as "the sale of at least five hundred product units during a month before one year after the funding date." Failure to sell five hundred product units in a month before that time would indicate to management and investors that the forecast was too optimistic, or that the sales department is not fully staffed.

As a rule, the financial projections contained in business plans make poor benchmarks because they are usually prepared long before unforeseen, but inevitable, problems arise. Since many business plans are prepared to attract investors, they tend to be optimistic in their assumptions. In fact, venture capitalists discount most company projections when they price a deal and do not really expect a company to meet all of the goals stated in their financial projections.

Nonetheless, business plan projections almost always provide a starting place for determining benchmarks. Some investors even try to impose benchmarks that are the same as the performance estimates contained in a company's projections. When this happens and the projections are not met, the unfortunate entrepreneur may find his investors released from future funding obligations, entitled to more company shares, or vested with greater control over company operations. To avoid these consequences, attempts to use business plan projections as benchmarks should be resisted vigorously, and conservative benchmarks should be used whenever possible. *See: Projections, Stage Financing.*

Blue Sky Laws refer to state statutes that prescribe the methods by which stocks and other securities may be sold or offered for sale within the state. As with the federal securities laws, these state statutes generally prohibit companies and shareholders from selling (or offering to sell) stocks and securities unless the sales are registered with the states' securities commissions or fit into one of the exemptions from registration provided by the states' blue sky statutes.

In most states, these exemptions parallel or complement many of the federal exemptions. Nevertheless, management should be certain, before offering or selling any securities, that the offer and sale will comply with the securities laws of the state in which the company is incorporated and in the states of residence (or formation) of each person (or entity) to whom the shares are offered or sold. Failure to comply with the requirements of applicable blue sky laws can subject a company and its principals to substantial liability. *See: Legend Stock, Private Placements, Reg D, Restricted Securities, Safe Harbors, SEC (Securities and Exchange Commission), 33 Act.*

Board Committees are groups made up of company directors who are assigned particular corporate responsibilities to oversee. In many companies, significant responsibilities, such as review and approval of executive compensation, are delegated to committees. Usually, the authority to establish committees is contained in the company's bylaws and the laws of the state in which the company is incorporated. Committees improve efficiency by giving management smaller groups of directors to work with on particular types of questions and by reducing the number of full-member board meetings that must be called.

The most common committees are audit committees, compensation committees, and stock committees. Audit committees set up and oversee auditing and accounting standards for a company and, thereby, establish the mechanisms by which management and the board monitor the operations of the company. The compensation and stock committees are often combined into one committee that establishes salaries for company employees and recommends the issuance of stock options to selected employees. Often the power of this committee includes the actual issuance of options within guidelines established by the board of directors.

The establishment of a stock committee without ensuring that the committee is properly constituted can create problems for a growing company. If the committee consists of one person, as is often the case, the company can find itself in trouble when it prepares to go public or merge with another company. This is because granting one person the power to issue options makes it too easy to inadvertently grant them to employees and others. And often, these unintended stock grants do not come to light until deals have been made to go public or merge.

In start-up situations, companies often find themselves short of cash and in desperate need to hire or keep qualified people. Without adequate cash, it can be difficult for a company to retain the people it needs. To bridge this gap, many companies issue shares or options to new and senior employees. The stock and options attract key people by giving them the opportunity to participate in the company's growth.

The problem with one-person stock committees, however, is that without the reservation of stock-granting power to a larger group, even casual conversations with employees about the desire to issue more stock or options can turn into legally binding obligations of the company. Given the intense pressures new companies and their employees face, the discussing of "more stock and more options" becomes commonplace. If the company president participates in these discussions and is the only person on the stock committee, they can easily lead to binding agreements to issue company stock.

To reduce this risk of inadvertent stock issuances, companies should avoid single-member stock committees so that stock and option grants require the approval of two or more persons before they become binding on the company. It is also helpful for the company's bylaws or board minutes to require options to be in writing and signed by all committee members. If company employees know this is the case, casual conversations are less likely to lead to misunderstandings. *See: Board of Directors, Going Public, ISOs (Incentive Stock Options), Stock Committee, Vesting Schedules.*

Board of Directors is the governing body of a corporation. It is elected by the shareholders and, in turn, elects the company's officers. The board of directors sets the direction of the company and oversees the activities of its officers. Investors often require a seat on a company's board of directors as a condition of funding.

The configurations of boards of directors vary greatly from company to company. Boards can consist of as few as one individual or as many persons as the company's bylaws permit the shareholders to elect. Many entrepreneurial companies have small boards consisting of the company's president or the president and one or two key shareholders. Others contain many members and include general business advisers, industry experts, and others with skills to lend to the company. The size and configuration of a company's board of directors usually depend in large part upon the founder's method of operation and the concessions he has had to make to raise money.

Company boards also differ in the degree to which they become involved in the management of a company. Some consult regularly with the company's officers and set specific directions for its operations. Others may meet regularly but function more as sounding boards for management, becoming involved only at the request of management and then usually only to approve a specific action. As with the size and configuration of a board, the method of its operation usually reflects the personalities of the individuals involved. If the company has a strong chief executive officer and profitable operations, the board may be relatively quiet. However, if the board members have a significant stake in the company's success, they may stay very active in the company even when it is doing well.

What's the best configuration for a growing company's board of directors? The answer depends in part upon the talents of the company's officers and its success in attracting outside board members who can add significantly to the company's prospects. As a general rule, however, smaller boards are easier to work with than larger ones and also tend to be more actively involved in the companies they represent. Too many members on a board can create inertia, making it difficult to call a board meeting and difficult for the board to arrive at a consensus when it does meet. As a result, entrepreneurs should try to keep their boards small, inviting only those people to serve as directors who have the interest and the time needed to devote to the company's affairs. Members should only be added to the board if they are required to complete a substantial funding or important contract, or if they can add significantly to the strength of the company. *See: Board Committees, Bylaws, Charter, Control, Cumulative Voting, Stock Committee.*

Boilerplate is a lawyer's word referring to "standard" terms and conditions contained in most financing agreements, but that are rarely negotiated when the major terms of a deal are discussed.

They are not, however, as standard or innocuous as many people believe (or would lead others to believe). In fact, boilerplate often consumes more than half of a financing agreement and contains important promises and representations made by the company and its principals. These promises and representations should be reviewed carefully, even if the tendency is to skip them because "they are just boilerplate."

One standard provision that appears in many financing agreements is the "accurate business plan" boilerplate. Its purpose is to assure the investor that management has not made any misrepresentations in its business plan. It usually appears in the representations and warranty section of the financing agreement and is a warranty of both the company and its management. It is a legitimate provision that can have very different effects depending on whose boilerplate is used. The provision sometimes appears as a representation that

> The business plan of the company is accurate and complete and does not contain any untrue statement or omit to state any fact which is necessary in order to make the statements contained therein not misleading.

A literal reading of this particular boilerplate can make company management a guarantor of the facts, assumptions, and conclusions contained in the business plan. If any of those facts, assumptions, and conclusions turn out to be untrue, the company and its management could wind up liable to the investor for damages. Since much of a business plan is based on "soft" information instead of hard, verifiable facts, and since much of it is judgmental and prospective, business plans almost always turn out to be untrue in some respect. And when they do, management making this representation may find itself surprised by the liability it has assumed.

A better boilerplate provision about the company's business plan, at least from management's perspective, would read

> To management's knowledge, the business plan does not contain any untrue statement of a material fact or omit to state a material fact that is necessary in order to make the statements contained therein not misleading in light of the circumstances under which they are made. To their knowledge, the financial projections contained in the business plan were prepared accurately based on the assumptions described therein.

This boilerplate gives the investor what he needs with less exposure to the company and its key officers. It talks in terms of knowledge instead of absolute facts and acknowledges that the projections are merely estimates based on disclosed assumptions. These differences can be important as a company's progress varies from its projected plans. For management, they can mean the difference between business as usual and defending a lawsuit brought by an investor.

Every lawyer has his own version of the "standard" boilerplate. Some are more exacting than others. All boilerplate terms are negotiable, notwithstanding any claims by their authors that they are "standard" or "required as is" in all of their deals. Management should never sign an agreement until it is comfortable with the boilerplate it contains. *See: Financing Agreements, Investment Reps, Reps and Warranties, We Always Do It This Way, We Never Exercise Our Rights Under This Section.*

Bricks and Mortar refers to a company's physical plant and facilities. Sometimes the phrase is used in a more general sense to refer to a company's tangible assets, such as land, buildings, machinery, and equipment. *See: Collateral, Nonrecourse Debt, Personal Guarantees.*

Bridge Loans are short-term financing agreements that fund a company's operations until it can arrange more comprehensive longer-term financing. The need for a bridge loan arises when a company runs out of cash before it can obtain more capital investment through long-term debt or equity.

Bridge loans are risky. Whether a company's original investors or an outside lender provides the bridge loan, its short-term nature creates pressure to complete the long-term financing package quickly. A default under a bridge loan usually gives the lender substantial rights to company assets or personal assets of management. Management's eagerness to liquidate a bridge loan can cause it to make concessions it would not otherwise agree to when negotiating the longer-term financing that will "take out" the bridge loan.

When accepting bridge financing, management should be careful to understand the consequences if the long-term financing does not come through on time. It helps to negotiate as long a term as possible on a bridge loan and to borrow enough money to carry the company through the loan's term. If the bridge loan is with an outside investor, management should explore the possibility of converting it into longer-term financing if the need arises, even if the terms of extending the bridge loan are less favorable than the anticipated terms of the "take-out" financing. Bridge loans should be documented. They should not be entered into until management has a clear written understanding of the main business terms of the company's total financing package. *See: Financing Agreements, Investment Memorandums, Letters of Intent, Leverage, Negotiation.*

Brokers are intermediaries who help companies and investors find one another. Many entrepreneurs hire brokers to help them raise money in the hope that by so doing, they will reduce the amount of time they will have to spend in fund-raising. For a busy entrepreneur, time spent raising money almost always takes time away from running the business.

In some cases, brokers can provide companies with valuable introductions that lead to financing. Some brokers can explain alternative sources of funding and help structure viable financing packages. Few, however, can completely replace management in the fund-raising process. Usually, the most they can do is provide management with introductions and a chance to "pitch" the company. Potential investors invariably want to deal directly with management. As a result, almost all entrepreneurs stay involved in the fund-raising process and continue to look for investors on their own, even when they hire a broker.

Entrepreneurs should be careful when dealing with a broker. They should make their agreements explicit and put them in writing. The agreements should define what the broker's responsibilities are, when he is entitled to a commission (usually when an investor he introduced to the company funds the company's needs), how much the commission will be, and when his assignment expires. To the extent possible, entrepreneurs should investigate the broker's reputation by talking with his present and former clients. They should also have explicit written understandings about the limits on the broker's authority to commit the company to any funding proposal.

Most brokers will work on a contingency fee or other prearranged fee basis. Whatever arrangements are made, however, management should understand that the broker's fee will often come out of management's pocket. Many investors will insist that money they put into a company go toward developing the company's product, not toward paying a broker.

Other professionals who can provide introductions and advice about finding money and structuring financing packages include bankers, accountants, lawyers, and— probably the best source — other entrepreneurs. *See: Consultants, CPAs (Certified Public Accountants), Due Diligence, Lawyers, Packages.*

Business Plan is a concise document, usually written by management, that describes a company, its products, business methods, financial condition, and needs for funding. Business plans are written to clarify company purposes, to plan new directions, and to raise capital from private investors. Often, business plans are written exclusively to raise money.

A good business plan should be concise, complete, and easy to understand. It should introduce a company and its objectives in a positive way that makes investors want to learn more about it. The content of the plan should show that management knows what it is doing. It should show that the company's management has the experience and talent necessary to make the company succeed.

Most venture capitalists insist on seeing a company's business plan before they will even consider an investment. The document's content gives them a basis upon which to evaluate their interest in a company. If the plan interests them, they will investigate further. If it does not, they will reject the company as a potential investment. Most venture capitalists see too many deals to spend time with companies whose business plans fail to excite them.

It is important, therefore, to prepare a business plan carefully and to make it easy to understand. Enough time should be allocated to writing and rewriting the plan so that it articulates clearly the excitement the company presents. At the same time, it must be well organized and carefully researched. Its discussion of the company and its industry should be based on thorough analysis. It should be thoughtful and realistic. After reviewing it, an investor should be excited about the company's prospects and impressed with management's preparation and candor.

There are many sources of help available to entrepreneurs who are preparing their first business plans. For example, accounting firms will often help prepare financial statements and projections. Some have professionals who will review a business plan and provide constructive criticism. Consultants can be used to conduct market research, assist at arriving at reasonable assumptions for projections, or help prepare parts of the plan. Other businessmen and lawyers will sometimes critique a business plan if asked.

For more information about business plans, entrepreneurs can check with accountants, lawyers, and other entrepreneurs. Many accounting firms have detailed brochures on how to prepare business plans that are available for the asking. Local bookstores and libraries also have valuable materials on business plans. *See: Brokers, Business Plan Format, Deal Flow, Downside, Due Diligence, Summary, Three Questions.*

The Writing of the Business Plan

Everyone talks about the importance of the business plan and they are correct to do so. Whether the plan is read by potential investors, friendly business associates or magazine editors, it represents the first opportunity to make an impression upon them. It will take lots of fancy footwork to overcome the bad impression created by a poor one. Therefore, when all else is said and done, your plan's key points should be abundantly clear. [Clear means easy to read, easy to understand, complete and accurate.] The authors of books on plan writing are right to point out all the details one should remember when constructing a plan, and the importance of a well-rehearsed presentation to accompany it.

However, no book on plan writing I have read focuses on one particular benefit that I have learned from several attempts at writing business plans: to write a clear plan, one must have a clear idea of the business being planned. And it is the process of writing that clarifies.

Long ago, in journalism school, I learned two axioms that kept occurring to me as I wrote the business plan for this publication: If You Can't Explain It, You Don't Understand It; and, Muddy Writing Reflects Muddy Thinking. As I wrote the plan for *VCCM (Venture's Capital Club Monthly)*, all the areas that I thought I could "fudge" became so apparent that the plan started to become farcical. At that point, I knew the only way the plan would get funded was for me to stop writing a plan and start planning a business. After that realization, the hard work really began, as I had no choice but to answer the questions I knew others would ask. Sure enough, readers asked questions about exactly what I knew was weak in the plan.

The process of writing itself benefits the business plan. Through the process of writing, the business becomes defined, its weaknesses become evident and demand to be rectified. As the plan goes through subsequent drafts, the thoughts of new readers can be included, so that the plan becomes consensual. By following the outline in many of the "How To" books, the gaps in your own thinking should emerge. As you gather the information necessary to respond to the suggested outline, your plan becomes denser, containing more of the stuff it is supposed to contain and you become more confident of the quality of the business.

Sales and financial projections were the hardest part for me. I resisted making projections in which I had no confidence, and yet I knew the plan was supposed to contain them. I resolved this dilemma three ways: (1) I did a lot of research to find "comparable" information; (2) I assigned probabilities to the projections, thus indicating those numbers where I had great certainty and those where I did not; and (3) I went ahead and made projections based on nothing but "feel," and when the time came, I admitted to "making the numbers up" where no data were available. I asked the readers to suggest sources of data I may have over looked. When no one could suggest a source, they were more understanding of the necessity to "plug" a number in.

My point is to appreciate the writing of the plan as a necessary thinking exercise, totally separate from the necessary fund-raising exercise. While you may hate to write at all, in this case it is unavoidable and you had better plunge in. Show your work around, don't be defensive about the criticism, re-draft to include good suggestions and anticipate the questions others will ask and include the answers.

One last thing: once you've written it, start updating it.

From a July 1985 Venture's Capital Club
Monthly *editorial by Steven Marshall Cohen*

Business Plan Format should allow a business plan to reflect management's thorough understanding of its company, its products, and its market. The organization of the plan should be apparent so that investors can find what they want quickly, without getting distracted by material that does not interest them. There are many formats an entrepreneur can follow when writing a business plan. The key is for the resulting plan to present the company's opportunity well. Here is an example of one acceptable format and the type of information investors expect each section in the plan to provide.

Sample Business Plan Format

Table of Contents

1. Summary
2. Company and industry
3. Products (or services)
4. The market
5. Marketing
6. Management
7. Development plan
8. Overall schedule
9. Risks
10. Financial statements and projections
11. Appendix

1. *Summary.* Investors expect a short summary of the important aspects of the company's proposal at the beginning of the plan. The summary should highlight the company's opportunity in a way that leaves no doubt in the reader's mind what the company has and what it needs to succeed. If the summary is confusing or poorly presented, the venture capitalist will probably read no further.

The summary should contain brief statements about

- The company's name, address, and telephone number.
- Who the investor should contact and how that person can be reached.
- The company's product and what distinguishes it from others in the market.
- A description of the company and its management team.
- Why the company's market is attractive.
- A summary of the company's financial projections.
- How much money the company needs and when it will need it.
- How the company will use the money.
- How the investor will get his money back.

It pays to write the summary first and to revise it several times. Have friends and business associates review this portion of the plan and ask them: Did it hold their interest? Did they understand what the company is making and why its product is unique? Did they remember how much outside capital management needs and how management intends to use it? Revise the summary if any of these points are missing or unclear.

2. *Company and industry.* This is the background section of the business plan. It should contain a concise history of the company, when it was formed, how management decided on its product, and what operations have been conducted. A brief description of the product and who its customers will be should also appear here.

This section should give management's analysis of the company's industry and the opportunity it provides to the company and its product. The company's competition in the market should be described. What are competitors doing and how will the company's strategy be different and better? If there are economic, technological, or social trends that management believes will affect the company and its market, they should be mentioned.

It is important for this section to be well researched. Venture investors will conduct a thorough review of the industry and of management's analysis of it. If the company's analysis appears shallow or unsophisticated, they will not invest.

Most investors will have their own views of the company's industry. They will not, however, know the industry from management's point of view or why management thinks the industry holds an opportunity for their company. If this section does not express the company's opportunity clearly, management should not be surprised if no one invests.

3. *Products (or services).* This section should contain a detailed description of the company's product. The description should emphasize what distinguishes its product from others in the marketplace. Diagrams and pictures can be used if they will help investors understand the product and what makes it distinctive.

The plan should be candid about the product's shortcomings as well as its strengths. Is it ready for market? Can it be easily copied? Will competitors bring out the next generation of the company's product soon? A venture capitalist will not expect the product to be perfect. If management pretends that it is, it will only make him suspicious. In being candid, however, it is also important to describe the product enthusiastically.

This section should describe whatever protection the product has from competition. If patented, the nature and importance of the patent should be explained. This may involve explaining why a particular patent claim is important to the distinctive features of the product, or why it would be difficult, costly, or time-consuming to engineer around the patent claim. If the protection of the product depends upon trade secrets or copyright protection, that should be explained.

Finally, if management knows what the company's next product will be, it should be mentioned here. Few products dominate a market for long. Venture capitalists realize this and like to know that management has given some thought to what comes next.

4. *The market.* This is an important and difficult part of the business plan. Here management must describe in detail why the market for the company's product is such that the company can expect to achieve its sales goals despite the existing competition. It is here that management must explain and justify its choice of marketing strategy.

In describing the market, management should identify the major buyers for the company's product. Are they more interested in price, quality, or features? How does the company's product meet these interests? The results of any research management has conducted with customers should be described. Are customers interested in the product at the company's price? If so, how concrete is their interest? If not, why not, and how does their lack of interest affect the company's plans?

Give the magnitude of the market the company is going after in whatever measurements are appropriate — units, revenues, etc. Who are the players? How much will the market expand, and how much of the market must the company capture to succeed? Describe in detail the factors that are moving the market and the direction in which it is going. Is the company's product positioned to take advantage of the trends?

Avoid overestimating the size and growth rate of the market. Base the company's estimates of market size and projections of market growth on discussions with potential customers, distributors, and competitors. Also, review the available market surveys, but do so critically. Markets change quickly, and the most respected market survey is often considered outdated by insiders.

Finally, evaluate the competition realistically. Evaluate competitors' products and their histories in the marketplace. Consider the market share and reputation for aggressiveness of each of the company's main competitors. Explain why potential customers buy from the company's competitors and why some of them will switch to a new supplier.

5. *Marketing.* This section should contain an analysis of the company's marketing strategy and projections of the unit sales management believes the company can achieve.

The company's marketing strategy should be explained in detail. The company's sales techniques and pricing policies should be described in relation to the distribution channels it will employ. How did management arrive at its pricing? How does that method compare with the pricing practices of the company's competitors?

What part will advertising play in the company's marketing? What type of advertising will be employed, and who will direct the effort? How will the company sell and distribute its product? Will it use a direct sales force, independent agents, or distributors? Discuss why management chose the sales and distribution channel it selected. Explain how management will organize the company's sales effort and how that effort will compare with that of its competitors.

6. *Management.* This section should contain résumés of the important members of the company's management team and describe what function each person will perform. The résumés should emphasize relevant experience, training, and education. Business accomplishments that illustrate the ability of management to make the company successful should be highlighted.

If the company's management team has weaknesses, as all do, discuss them candidly and describe what plans management has for overcoming these weaknesses. Also, describe briefly the accounting, legal, advertising, banking, and other professional relationships the company has established.

7. *Development plan.* This is the section in which management discusses how it will go about achieving the company's objectives. What is the current status of the company's product? If it requires development work, who will do it? Will the company use an outside design house for some of the work? If company employees will do the work, are they all on board, or does management still have to locate key personnel?

The development plan should describe the company's requirements for space, facilities, equipment, and personnel. Will the company begin manufacturing immediately or contract out manufacturing at first? If the company will do some assembly work or testing, explain why and how. Describe who the company's suppliers will be and how management will control quality, production, and inventory.

8. *Overall schedule.* This schedule should show when management plans to accomplish each of the milestones that is critical to the company's success. A well-considered and realistic schedule demonstrates management's ability to plan the company's growth. It also displays management's

ability to identify the critical tasks to be achieved by the company and how they interrelate.

This section should contain a flow chart analysis that shows the timing of the company's product development and operational activities and when the company plans to meet the important thresholds in its marketing plans. Some of the events management might cover include

- When the company was incorporated.
- When the management team will be completed.
- When the company's product prototype will be finished.
- When the company will complete product testing.
- When the company will begin producing products for sale.
- When products will be offered for sale.
- When the company will begin receiving orders.
- When the company will make its first deliveries.
- When the company will begin receiving payments for products shipped.

The schedule might also show

- When the company will need money and in what amounts.
- When trade shows or exhibitions are scheduled.
- When and what additional people will need to be hired.
- When the company will need to add new facilities or significant amounts of equipment.

Be realistic in the schedule. Follow it with a narrative discussion of those events that are most likely to be delayed and how those delays could affect the company's overall schedule. Also, explain what management can do to make up for any schedule slippage that occurs.

9. *Risks.* Every venture capitalist knows that new businesses are risky. They may not, however, understand which risks are most dangerous to the company or how management intends to neutralize them. This section enables management to discuss those risks and how it plans to overcome them. By doing this thoroughly, management increases its credibility with investors and demonstrates its foresight. Some risks that might be discussed include

- Risks that relate to the industry.
- Risks associated with not obtaining financing on schedule.
- Risks of not meeting the development schedule or the product cost estimates.
- Risks that competitors may develop new, more competitive products.
- Risks that essential personnel cannot be located or retained.

Every major risk of which management is aware should be addressed. Nothing is gained by omitting important items from the list of risk factors.

10. *Financial statements and projections.* This section should contain historical financial statements of the company's operations and projections of future operations. The projections should be for a period of three to five years. They should include profit-and-loss forecasts, cash flow projections, and pro forma balance sheets broken out on a monthly basis.

Narrative explanations should accompany the financial projections, with important facts and assumptions contained in the projections highlighted, along with conclusions management wants the investor to draw.

11. *Appendix.* The appendix should supplement the business plan and support management's conclusions. Use the appendix to attach résumés of key management members when those résumés elaborate on relevant experiences. Copies of key contracts or commitments from suppliers and customers that demonstrate the viability of the company's product or concept can be included. If there are any surveys or studies that emphasize the company's good prospects or explain a key concept, photocopies of relevant portions of those surveys can help an investor understand the company better. *See: Brokers, Business Plan, Downside, Due Diligence, Exits, Five Factors, Market Research, Packages, Projections, Summary, Three Questions.*

Buy-Sell Agreements are contracts that entitle one shareholder to force others either to buy his stock or to sell him theirs. These contracts often appear as provisions in a financing or shareholders' agreement.

Many investors insist on buy-sell agreements with the managements of companies they fund. They view these agreements as a way to help them withdraw from a company that does not live up to their expectations. With a buy-sell, investors know they can either get their money out or get management's shares. With management's shares, they can usually replace management or have enough shares to sell control of the company to others.

Buy-sell agreements usually work like this: Two or more shareholders agree that if the company fails to meet certain goals, either may buy all of the other's stock in the company. By the terms of the agreement, whichever shareholder exercises this option must first offer to sell his stock to the other shareholder. The purchase price per share is usually the same for both shareholders (although sometimes the price is slightly lower for management). In this way, either shareholder can force the other out of the company but only by risking being bought out himself.

In practice, buy-sell agreements often work to remove management. This is because they are usually exercised only when the company is not living up to expectations. In these circumstances, it can be hard for management to raise enough money to buy out the investor. Even when management succeeds in raising the money, it often does so only by selling more stock to a new investor than it purchases from the old one. This reduces management's percentage in the company.

When management cannot raise the money, it loses its stock and its control of the company. If management has given personal guarantees to secure company borrowings, management not only loses its interest in the company but also remains bound to its guarantees. Because many new company borrowings require guarantees, management should be sure that any buy-sell agreement it signs requires the investor to get management released from any personal guarantees it has made for the company. Otherwise, management may remain liable for its guarantees while the company's ability to repay its loans is determined by how well others (that is, new management) manage the company.

Whenever a buy-sell agreement is required by an investor, management should try to structure the agreement in ways that reduce the investor's ability to exercise the buy-sell and increase the chance that the investor, and not management, will be the party that sells. The best way to keep a buy-sell silent is to make its exercise contingent on the company failing to meet goals that are easily attainable. As long as these goals are met, the investor has no right to force a buy-sell on management. Making the purchase price lower for management can discourage an investor's exercise by forcing him to give management a bargain or pay a premium himself. The lower price makes it easier for management to buy out the investor and stay in control.

Giving management the right to use promissory notes for part of the purchase price helps, too, by making it easier for management to pay for the investor's shares. So does giving management a long time in which to respond to the investor's offer. It is much easier to raise $500,000 in 120 days than in 30 days. Finally, buy-sell agreements should expire if they are not exercised within a fixed period of time. The shorter the period the better.

Buy-sell agreements, when funded by insurance, are also used by company owners to provide liquidity for their estates and orderly transitions for their companies when one of the owners dies. These buy-sell agreements, because the buy-out is funded by insurance and because the sale is triggered only by an owner's death, provide none of the potential inequities described above. Care must be taken with these agreements to provide assurances of continuing insurance coverage and mechanisms for adjusting price to reflect future share values. *See: Co-Sale Agreements. Exits, First Refusal Rights, Liquidity Agreements, Puts, Shareholders' Agreements, Unlocking Provisions.*

Bylaws are the operating rules of a corporation. They are adopted by the company's board of directors and govern such things as the election of directors, the size of the board of directors, and the election and function of each of the company's officers. Bylaws can normally be amended by the company's directors and are more easily changed than the company's charter, which can only be amended with shareholder approval. *See: Charter, Directors' Indemnities.*

C

Calls are a company's contractual rights to require a shareholder to surrender shares of company stock in return for payment of an agreed-upon sum of money. Calls are usually contingent upon the happening of some future event, such as the passage of time or the accomplishment of some goal by the company.

Management might exercise a call and redeem an investor's stock if another investor was willing to pay a higher price for shares than the call price. Even without a ready investor, management might call an investor's stock if it believed the market value of the company's stock had risen to more than the call price. In each case, redeeming stock at a call price that is below market value can increase the value of the remaining shareholders' stock.

The cost to the company is the cash required to pay the investor for his shares. In deciding to exercise a call, management must weigh the potential benefit of redeeming shares at below market prices against the company's need for the cash used to exercise the call and its ability to replace that cash when needed.

Calls are usually optional but can, by express agreement, be made mandatory. A mandatory call, however, is nothing more than a contract to redeem stock. As with a put (which entitles a shareholder to force a company to redeem shares), an obligation to exercise a call should be conditioned on the company's ability to meet the corporate law requirements of the company's state of incorporation.

These laws often restrict the types of funds a company can legally use to redeem shares. *See: Cash Flow, Exits, Puts.*

Cash Flow is the money coming into (actually received) and going out of (actually disbursed) a business. The three main sources of cash coming into a company are product sales, stock sales, and borrowing. Operating expenses (for example, payroll), capital expenditures (for example, equipment purchases), and debt service on borrowed money (interest and principal payments) account for most of the cash going out.

Having enough money coming into a company to meet its obligations to pay money out is critical to its success. Venture capitalists are very interested in whether a company will have sufficient cash flow and are very sophisticated in analyzing a company's need for cash. Most investors will study a company's monthly cash flow projections carefully before making an investment decision.

Inadequate cash flow can cause acute problems for any business. A shortage of cash can create a series of crises that divert management from the crucial business of running the company to the business of searching for "new" money. Cash flow problems quickly become visible to suppliers and competitors and can be used by them to suggest to customers that the company is unstable and, therefore, unreliable. The damage such suggestions can cause, even if unfounded, is considerable.

For a company anticipating rapid growth, the problems can be compounded. Fast growth, even with growing profits, can put extreme pressures on a company's available cash. Growing sales are usually accompanied by demands for cash that grow faster than the growth in cash receipts. This is due, in part, to the fact that more sales create more receivables before they create more cash receipts. At the same time, demands for payment from suppliers grow, and other new expenditures must be made to support the growth. Many of these expenditures cannot be delayed. The mistiming of the receipt of funds and their disbursement can become so severe that profitable expansions must be postponed. Because of this possibility, companies should thoroughly analyze and review their anticipated cash flow needs regularly, even when they are not searching for capital. *See: Debentures, Debt Service, Equity, Leverage.*

Cashing Out (or In) refers to a shareholder selling his shares of company stock for cash, and thus realizing his return (or his loss). It is a term near and dear to the hearts of investors when it refers to a profitable sale of shares. Cashing out at a loss is even preferable in many cases to holding stock in a declining company, particularly when the stock is illiquid because of restrictions on its resale. Cashing out can be accomplished in a variety of ways, including going public, exercising a put, or transferring shares to a new investor. *See: Buy-Sell Agreements, Calls, Convertible Securities, Co-Sale Agreements, Demand Rights, Exits, Going Public, Liquidity Agreements, Piggyback Rights, Puts, Registration Rights.*

CDCs (Community Development Corporations) are governmental or quasi-governmental agencies that lend and invest in companies that locate in their communities. They are often affiliated with local municipalities or economic development agencies.

CDCs review investments and conduct due diligence as other investors do. But because of their interest in community development, they often consider factors that do not interest traditional venture capitalists, such as the employment opportunities and tax revenues the proposed business will generate for the community. Businesses that meet a community need can often secure funding from a CDC when other investors might not be interested. And the funding they secure is sometimes at lower rates and for longer terms than other sources will provide. This is because of the special investment criteria CDCs have relating to job and tax generation, which enable them to justify lower returns on investment and longer-term loans. *See: BDCs (Business Development Corporations), Corporate Venture Capital, Due Diligence, ROI (Return on Investment), Venture Capitalists.*

Charter is the document that enfranchises a corporation. It is sometimes called "articles of incorporation" and is usually filed with the secretary of state in the state in which the company incorporates. The charter spells out what activities the corporation may undertake, the number and type of shares of capital stock it is authorized to issue, and the names of the company's founding members. As a general rule, the charter can only be amended by a vote of the shareholders. Often a vote of two-thirds of the shares is required. An example of a simple charter is provided below. *See: Bylaws.*

Sample Charter

Imaginary Newco Inc.
Articles of Incorporation

> The undersigned, being a natural person of the age of at least 18 years and acting as sole incorporator to organize a corporation (the "Corporation") under the provisions of the Georgia Business Corporation Code,

does hereby adopt and sign the following Articles of Incorporation:

I.
Name

The name of the Corporation is Imaginary Newco Inc.

II.
Authority

The Corporation is organized pursuant to the provisions of the Georgia Business Corporation Code.

III.
Duration

The period of duration of the Corporation is perpetual.

IV.
Purpose

The nature of the business and the purpose to be conducted and promoted are to buy, sell and generally deal in products which are imaginary; and to engage in any lawful act or activity for which corporations may be incorporated under the Georgia Business Corporation Code and to exercise all the rights, privileges, immunities, and authority granted to or exercised by business corporations under the laws of the state of Georgia now in effect or that will become effective during the existence of this Corporation.

V.
Capitalization

The aggregate number of shares of stock which the Corporation shall have authority to issue is 10,000, all of the par value of $.01 each. All such shares are of one class and are designated as Common Stock.

VI.
Minimum Consideration

The Corporation will not commence business until consideration of at least $500.00 has been received by the Corporation for the issuance of shares.

VII.
Denial of Preemptive Rights

No holder of any shares of any class of the Corporation shall be entitled as a right to subscribe for, purchase, or otherwise acquire (a) any shares of any class of the Corporation which the corporation proposes to issue, (b) any rights or options which the Corporation proposes to grant for the purchase of any shares of any class of the Corporation, or (c) any bonds, securities or obligations of the Corporation which the Corporation proposes to issue or grant which are convertible into or exchangeable for, or which carry any right to subscribe for, purchase, or otherwise acquire, any shares of any class of the Corporation.

VIII.
Capital Surplus

The Corporation may make distributions to its shareholders out of its capital surplus and purchase its own shares out of its unreserved and unrestricted capital surplus upon such terms and conditions as the Board of Directors shall deem appropriate.

IX.
Registered Agent and Office

The address of the initial registered office of the Corporation is 1040 Crown Pointe Parkway, Suite 800, Atlanta, Georgia 30338, and the name of the initial registered agent at such address is Clinton Richardson.

X.
Directors

The number of directors constituting the initial Board of Directors of Imaginary Newco Inc. shall be one and the name and address of such director is as follows:

Ann McArthur
Imagination Lane
Atlanta, Georgia 30335

XI.

Incorporator

The name and address of the incorporator are as follows:

William Francis
55 Park Place
Suite 400
Atlanta, Georgia 30335

In Witness Whereof, the undersigned executes these Articles of Incorporation this 1st day of January, 1993.

William Francis
Incorporator

Cheap Stock is a securities term referring to corporate shares that are priced below the price of an anticipated public offering. A number of states impose restrictions on stock issued to company promoters when the company conducts a public offering. These states generally consider cheap stock to be that issued to company promoters within three years for less than the public offering price. If the state securities commission finds the founders' stock to be cheap stock, it may impose escrow requirements on the founders' stock as a condition of the company conducting its offering in that state. While these escrow requirements can be waived in certain circumstances, the net effect is often to reduce the number of states in which a company conducts its offering and to deprive the residents of states that are excluded of the opportunity to consider investing in a new company's public offering. *See: Bargain Stock, Blue Sky Laws, Going Public.*

Closing is when all of the agreements between investor and entrepreneur are completed and the signing of documents occurs. Immediately thereafter, the investor begins funding the company. The agreements signed at a venture capital financing are usually referred to as financing agreements. These agreements govern the ongoing relationship between the investor and the entrepreneur.

Closings are usually a time of excitement and high expectations. In most instances, closings follow a long process of negotiation, document preparation and revision, and personal stress. A sense of euphoria accompanies most closings, and often the entrepreneur rushes out after the closing to make long-delayed expenditures for the company. These expenditures, if planned, can help the company grow and lead it to its next round of success. If made impetuously, however, they can lead to wasted expectations and the realization that the expensive fundraising process must begin again before it should have. *See: Financing Agreements.*

How to Care for an Entrepreneurial Investor— After You Cash His Check

Intelligent information transfer and timely communication are my prescriptions for a continuing happy (or at least satisfactory), healthy and nondestructive investor/entrepreneur relationship. What I mean is very simple. The entrepreneur should prepare the investor for realism, frequently spelled the same as disappointment.

Specifically, the entrepreneur should establish a regularly scheduled series of communication elements with the investor(s). These communication elements should be both written and personal. I am a strong believer that monthly newsletters with charts should be sent to investors. The charts should be the reflections of a living business plan. The charts display previously achieved results, current period results, and projected results as well as new or amended projections.

The entrepreneur should meet with the investor at least quarterly, and probably monthly, for the purpose of keeping the investor within the family and delaying, for as long as possible, the development of the "we v. they" syndrome. Once the we/they thinking has developed and the camps become established, the problems begin. The entrepreneur should do everything possible to have the investor play a role which keeps him feeling that he is on the entrepreneur's team and is in fact making a contribution. If the problems of the company in achieving objectives are fully and fairly understood by the investor and he feels that he is on the team, he will possibly be available for additional funding and certainly not be resentful of the need for it.

Entrepreneurs can ask their investors to help: Help to gain information, help to gain customers, help with public relations and, on occasion, help with personnel matters. The entrepreneur should recognize that in most cases the investor had to have been competent in some areas of activity which are, or can be, useful to the entrepreneur's company to have made the money which he has invested. A knowledge of the investor's strengths should be in the entrepreneur's asset file.

From an article by Arthur Lipper, III,
author of Financing and Investing in Private Companies

Collateral is any asset pledged as security for a loan. If a collateralized loan is not repaid as agreed, the creditor can call upon the collateral to secure repayment. By reducing the lender's risk, collateral makes it easier for a company to borrow and to borrow at a favorable rate. In contrast to bank loans, which are often collateralized, most venture capital investments are made with little or no collateral.

Available collateral should not be ignored. With traditional lenders, it can decrease the risk and thereby increase the principal amount lent to the company. Collateral can also reduce the interest rate charged for the loan. By making borrowed funds available to a company, collateral can delay the need for expensive venture capital and the dilution of management's stock ownership that occurs when an equity investment is made. Also, collateral can be used to secure portions of a venture capital investment that is structured as debt and thereby make the capital easier to attract. *See: Dilution (Percentage), Equity, Factoring, Inventory Financing, Nonrecourse Debt.*

Commitment is what venture capitalists look for in an entrepreneur. They want to invest only in companies whose management is 100 percent committed to the company's success. Venture capitalists want management's full-time attention.

Starting a new business is an exhausting and all-consuming endeavor. Entrepreneurs often work more than twelve hours a day, day after day, seeing to all the details that make a company succeed. Weekend work is common. In the process, family relationships can suffer. Investors understand this. They want to know that the entrepreneur and his family understand as well and are prepared to make the sacrifices required.

Investors also expect entrepreneurs to take their companies as far as they can with their own resources. Investors do not like entrepreneurs who hedge their financial bets on their companies. If they invest their money, investors want to know that entrepreneurs have invested their money as well. Entrepreneurs who retain a safety net of cash outside the company make some investors nervous and thereby reduce the likelihood of receiving funding. *See: Entrepreneur, Ethics, Zeal.*

Commitment Letters are documents issued by lenders to companies after they have decided to make loans but before they are ready to complete the formal loan documents. Commitment letters are usually short and describe only the essential terms of the pending loan.

Most commitment letters obligate the lender to make the described loan only if the company meets all of the conditions identified in the letter. Once the conditions are met, the commitment is further documented with more complete (lengthy) loan, security, and guarantee agreements that contain many terms and conditions not specified in the commitment letter.

Commitment letters serve a useful purpose. By setting out the general terms of the loan, they solidify each party's commitment to move forward with the deal. They also ensure that the parties have, in fact, come to terms with one another on the major points of the deal.

Commitment letters should not be treated lightly. They should be reviewed as carefully as the final, formal loan documents they precede. Even though many of their provisions may not be legally binding (at least until all the conditions are met), some may be enforceable against the company in any event. Also, these letters set the tone for how negotiations of the formal loan agreements will proceed. Both parties will expect the deal to be completed in the manner set out in the letter. As a result, it can be very difficult to negotiate and close a loan that includes terms significantly different from those contained in an earlier commitment letter. *See: Bridge Loans, Investment Memorandums, Letter Agreements, Letters of Intent.*

Common Stock is what most people think of when they think of owning part of a company. It is the security most frequently issued by companies and represents an ownership interest in a company. In most cases, common stock carries the right to vote for directors and to vote on other matters affecting the company. It also entitles holders to receive notice of shareholder meetings and to attend them. Rights to review corporate records or receive financial reports also customarily accompany common stock ownership. Certificates are usually issued to holders of common stock (and other company securities) to evidence the stock's existence.

Common stock can pay cash dividends based on company earnings, but only after preferred stockholders receive their dividends. Dividends are usually paid at the discretion of the company's board of directors but are the exception, not the rule, with most growing, privately held companies. Holders of common stock participate last in company liquidations. Company creditors, debenture holders, and preferred stockholders get paid in that order, before holders of common stock.

Common stock can be issued in one or more classes. One frequently used company structure authorizes the issuance of two classes of common stock, which differ only in the number of directors each class is entitled to elect. This arrangement can be used to ensure an investor a seat on a company's board of directors while, at the same time, ensuring that control of the board will remain with management. For example, Class A stock might be issued to management and give its holders the right to elect three directors. Class B stock, which entitles its holders to elect only one director, is then issued to the investor. Even if the investor holds twice as many shares of stock as the Class A shareholders do, he can still elect only one director. In this way, even if management holds less than half of the company's stock, it can still control the company and its board of directors. *See: Board of Directors, Control, Cumulative Voting, Debentures, Equity, Junior Common Stock, Options, Preferred Stock, S Corporations.*

Compensation and Bonus Plans are company policies that provide money or other benefits to company officers and selected employees in excess of their salaries.

Most companies seeking venture capital cannot afford fancy compensation and bonus plans, particularly those that require cash. At the same time, however, growing companies need incentives to attract and keep valuable employees. In many instances, they need their key employees more than their established competitors need theirs. This is because the smaller size of the entrepreneurial company makes each employee more important. Unfortunately, though, the entrepreneurial status of the company also means less job security and, usually, lower salaries.

To offset these hiring disadvantages, most start-up companies use their stock and its relatively low market value. They do so by offering important employees the opportunity to acquire equity in the company. The attraction for the employee is the chance to purchase large quantities of stock at low prices in anticipation of the company growing and the stock increasing in value.

Young companies take advantage of their cheap stock by fashioning compensation and bonus plans around the right to acquire shares of company stock. The most widely used plans are ones that allow key employees to purchase company stock or acquire options to purchase it in the future.

Often, the grants of stock or options are conditioned in ways that encourage the employee to remain with the company after the stock is purchased. For instance, shares of stock purchased pursuant to a plan may not "vest" immediately. Instead, they may vest over a period of years. During that period the company may have an option or obligation to repurchase the unvested shares from the employee at cost if he leaves the company for any reason.

The company may even have rights to repurchase a departing employee's vested shares for some predetermined price. All of these conditions are designed to reward employees who stay by increasing their ownership in the company and to penalize those who leave.

With stock option grants, the company may make them exercisable at today's low prices but contingent upon some future event. The employee's right to purchase shares may be restricted until he has been with the company for a year or until the company attains certain sales goals. Once the conditions are met, the employee can purchase the stock until the option's expiration date. If the conditions are not met, the option dies and the employee gets no stock.

Other common plans include issuing "phantom stock" and granting options to purchase special classes of stock. Grants of stock bonuses to employees from a pool of shares set aside for that purpose are used also. The variety of plans available to attract important employees is limited only by the imaginations of management and its advisers. A good adviser can help management select an incentive plan (or plans) that reward employees in ways that secure their attention, enthusiasm, and tenure with the firm. *See: Golden Handcuffs, ISOs (Incentive Stock Options), Junior Common Stock, Phantom Stock Plans, Stock Committee, Vesting Schedules.*

Confidentiality Agreements are contracts used to protect trade secrets and know-how from being misused or misappropriated by those who have access to them. When these agreements are used, they can help companies prevent competitors from learning valuable secrets. For many start-up and technology-based companies, the secrets these agreements help protect are among the most valuable properties they have. Often, those secrets constitute the essential difference between them and their competitors.

Having written contracts that obligate employees to maintain the secrecy of a company's techniques, processes, or know-how can mean the difference between maintaining a competitive advantage or giving it away to competitors.

In some cases, confidentiality agreements can even cover "negative know-how." That is, they can prohibit the transfer of information about mistakes the company made in perfecting its technology or project, information many would not normally think of as secret or important. Restricting negative know-how, however, can help ensure that a company's competitors will have the opportunity to make the same time-consuming mistakes the company made, and thereby delay the introduction of competitive products.

State laws generally permit companies to prevent others from using their secrets only as long as they treat the secrets as confidential and take reasonable precautions to prevent them from being disclosed to others. Depending upon the nature of the secrets, these necessary precautions might include restricting access to confidential data or setting aside a safe or room for storage of secret documents.

In most cases, written confidentiality agreements should also be required from everyone who has access to company secrets. The importance of these agreements and of complying with the company's other secrecy procedures should be impressed upon new employees and consultants. Employees who are departing should be reminded of their secrecy agreements. No one should be given access to a company secret before he signs a confidentiality agreement.

No venture capitalist wants to invest in a company that has not taken steps to protect its valuable secrets. Most will carefully review a company's arrangements to protect its secrets. And most will expect management and other company employees to be bound by written confidentiality agreements. Many will engage local counsel to be sure the agreements are enforceable. Because of this and the fact that the state laws that govern the enforceability of these agreements vary widely and are quite specific in their requirements, care should be taken when drafting a confidentiality agreement. To be sure of its enforceability, it should be prepared or reviewed by experienced legal counsel. *See: Employment Contracts, Patents, Software Protection, Think Capital, Trade Secrets.*

Consultants are professionals who perform specific services on behalf of company management for a fee. Many start-ups hire consultants to obtain specific expertise and to delay the expense of hiring additional full-time employees. Consultants do not earn fringe benefits, as employees do, and thus can be less expensive in the short run. They can also be hired by task and thereby be used when a full-time employee would not be economical.

One common use of consultants is to assist in the preparation of a business plan. Another is to assist in conducting market research or to advise in developing a company's product, manufacturing process, or marketing strategy. Sometimes, companies hire persons to consult whom they are interested in hiring full-time in the future. This allows the company to get services it needs and evaluate a person for staff employment at the same time. (As with company employees, consultants should always be required to sign confidentiality agreements when they are given access to company secrets.) Consultants' services can be paid for in a variety of ways.

Consultants who are hired to help raise money should be used carefully. Regardless of their claims, do not expect them to replace management entirely in the fund-raising process. Even with the best consultant or broker, investors will want to meet and measure management's knowledge of its business plan and its ability to make the company succeed. The only way investors can do this is if management participates actively in the preparation of the business plan and in discussions with investors. *See: Brokers, Consulting Agreements.*

Consulting Agreements are contracts between companies and advisers who are not their employees. Whenever practical, these agreements should be in writing. Good agreements should set out the scope of the consultant's obligations, understandings as to who owns his work product, and his fee arrangement. If the consultant's duties give him access to company secrets, the agreement should contain secrecy provisions. If they require him to interact with company customers or suppliers, the limitations on his authority should be carefully delineated.

Some investors require companies to enter into consulting agreements with them as a condition of funding. These contracts usually require the company to pay a monthly or quarterly fee to the investor for advice management might obtain anyway by virtue of its relationship with the investor. The real purpose of many of these consulting agreements is to increase the investor's return and give him access to management. Investors who require consulting agreements often tie the consulting fees to their cost of monitoring the company. Some investors believe consulting agreements improve their communication with management. They argue that managements feel fewer reservations about asking for investor advice when they are paying for it.

The fee paid for investor consulting services increases the company's cost of capital and decreases its available cash. Whenever possible, these consulting agreements and their fees should be avoided. When avoiding them is not possible, the consulting fee should be reviewed carefully and included in the company's calculation of its true cost of capital. *See: Cash Flow, Consultants, Financing Agreements, Management Agreements, Pricing.*

Control is the ability to direct the actions of a company. It includes the power to determine company strategy and to select the people who will carry out that strategy. In a corporation, control consists of the ability to elect or persuade a majority of the board of directors. Control can be ensured through ownership of enough shares of stock to elect more than half of the company's directors. In most cases, this means owning more than 50 percent of the company's voting stock.

Raising capital affects management's control in several ways. When enough stock to elect a majority of a company's board of directors is sold, management continues to direct the company only as long as the investors consent. Even when less stock is sold, contractual provisions required by an investor as a condition to funding can also change control by reducing management's unrestricted freedom to run the company. These provisions usually entitle the investor to participate in certain management decisions and to receive detailed and regular financial reports. Some contractual rights affect control by giving investors the right to manage the company if performance standards are not achieved.

As a rule, venture capitalists are more interested in obtaining high rates of return on their investments than in obtaining control of companies. Most want control only to the extent that they believe is necessary to protect their investments. Few are interested in running the day-to-day affairs of a company.

Even when an investor acquires the ability to elect a majority of a company's board, there are ways management can retain operating control. A shareholders' agreement requiring the investor to vote his stock for a slate of directors that is controlled by management is one example. Management contracts are another. These can be used to ensure management of at least minimum representation on the company's board of directors or of the right to direct the company's activities as long as it does so within agreed-upon parameters.

Classes of common stock can also be created to ensure that control stays with management. By issuing a second class of common stock to the investors that only has the right to elect a minority of the company's directors, management can retain majority control of the company's board of directors even when it sells a majority of the company's outstanding capital. A combination of these devices can be used to keep control of the board of directors in management's hands.

Most investors insist on some influence over a company's affairs as a condition of funding and require a seat on the company's board of directors. Few will want to control the board unless they lack confidence in management's abilities. Most will expect to receive regular financial reports from company management.

Investors will say that they are not interested in control. They will say that as long as management runs the company successfully they will not interfere. Nonetheless, management's definition of success may differ significantly from that of its investors. And investors may develop independent reasons for moving a company in a direction that does not interest management. The only way for management to ensure its control is through ownership of enough stock to elect a majority of the company's board of directors or through a binding written agreement with the investors. *See: Affirmative Covenants, Board of Directors, Common Stock, Cumulative Voting, Management Agreements, Negative Covenants, Operating Covenants, Shareholders' Agreements, Take Away Provisions, Voting Agreements, Voting Trusts.*

Convertible Debentures are debt instruments which entitle the lender to exchange the right to receive principal and interest payments into stock of the borrowing company. *See: Convertible Securities, Debentures.*

Convertible Preferred Stock is a type of stock used frequently by venture capital investors. The stock's preferred status gives the investor a preference in the event of a company liquidation or sale and often requires the company to pay dividends to the investor. A typical convertible preferred stock used by a venture capitalist also entitles the investor to convert his shares into common stock at a predetermined formula and to vote the preferred stock on issues presented for shareholder vote. The conversion formula includes adjustment mechanisms that protect the investor against unfair dilution by sales of cheaper stock to later investors. Most convertible preferred stocks also permit the investor to require the company to redeem the preferred stock after a predetermined time for an amount that gives the investor a modest profit. *See: Convertible Securities, Preferred Stock Umbrella, Structure.*

Convertible Securities are equity or debt investments that can be exchanged for something else of value upon the happening of some future event. The most common convertible securities are debentures and preferred stock that are convertible into common stock. The election of the holder is usually all that is required to convert.

Convertible securities are a nice way for investors to hedge. They allow them to acquire a debt instrument, with its rights to interest and principal payments, without sacrificing the chance to participate in the company's capital appreciation. When a company does well, the investor can convert his debenture into stock that is more valuable. When a company is less successful, he can retain his debenture and receive his interest and principal payments.

Most venture capitalists like convertible securities because they help preserve their capital and give them the potential of profiting from increases in the value of the company's stock. By giving their holders an option for removing money from a modestly successful company, convertible securities help investors preserve their capital even when their portfolio companies are not successful enough to allow them to liquidate their investments through public offerings. Contrary to popular opinion, most venture capital investments do not generate large profits for their investors. Most portfolio companies succeed modestly or fail. Deal structures that include convertible debentures can enable investors to retrieve their capital from their modest successes for reinvestment in other companies. *See: Cashing Out (or In), Convertible Preferred Stock, Debentures, Downside, Equity, Liquidity Agreements, Upside.*

Copyrights are protections afforded to writing by federal law. They prevent unauthorized copying or duplicating of protected works. The protections are available to writings of all kinds, including computer software.

Copyrights protect the expression of ideas and are often contrasted with trade secret protection, which protects ideas themselves but not their expression. The distinctions are important.

Companies cannot publish their secret processes in a magazine with a copyright notice and expect to keep others from using the processes. The copyright will prevent only the duplication of the way in which those ideas were expressed in the magazine. By the same token, there are things such as mass-marketed video games and monitor displays for which copyrights provide valuable protections that trade secrets cannot. And, where the use of a secret process requires copying of the expression of that process, as with most computer software programs, copyrights can, for many practical purposes, protect the process itself.

Copyrights can be obtained for computer software in object code or source code. They can also be obtained for documentation, manuals, and display screen configurations. Copyrights are available to software that is mass-marketed or sold under restrictive license.

Securing copyright protection requires careful compliance with federal copyright rules. Whenever copyrights are used to protect a valuable asset, companies should engage qualified counsel to assist them in making the application. Particularly when the asset is software, management should understand the advantages and disadvantages to copyrights and the best application procedure to follow before sending a program printout to Washington. Qualified lawyers can help management determine whether copyrights, trade secrets, or a combination of the two is the best protection for a company's asset. They can also plot a strategy for obtaining those protections. *See: Software Protection, Trade Secrets.*

Corporate Venture Capital refers to the fact that many large corporations have separate subsidiaries that make venture investments. These corporations often focus their investments, like specialty funds, on companies within certain industries.

Corporate venture companies evaluate investment proposals in much the same way as do traditional venture capitalists. They conduct extensive due diligence and look for a high rate of return from their investments. In addition, venture corporations frequently look for companies and products that can fill a market niche the corporation's parent wants to enter or that can develop technology the parent needs.

Corporate venture capitalists can make good partners for companies with good products who need assistance in marketing them. Often, the corporate partner can lend its marketing expertise and give the company access to distribution channels that accelerate its growth. Sometimes a corporate partner can lend technological assistance to a company as well. Because they are often able to provide some specific strategic assistance, managements should explore the additional "value added" the corporate investor can bring to the table and contract in the financing agreement for those investor services the company needs. *See: Joint Ventures, Specialty Funds, Value Added, Venture Capitalists.*

Corporations are a favorite form of business entity used extensively by small and large companies. Chartered by any one of the 50 states, corporations afford their owners and operators with limited liability in most situations and provide clear mechanisms for business management. Owned by shareholders who elect a board of directors to direct management, corporations are operated day-to-day by officers who are appointed by the board.

The most common form of corporation is the C corporation, which is taxed as a separate entity and whose shareholders are not taxed until they receive distributions, commonly called dividends, from the company. Since the corporation is separately taxed on its earnings, any dividends received by its shareholders are effectively taxed twice. For example, $1 of earnings would be taxed by the corporation at its rate, say 25 percent, leaving $.75 in after-tax earnings. If that $.75 is distributed to shareholders, it will be taxed again to the shareholder at his rate, say 33 percent, leaving $.50 of the original earnings after tax.

S corporations are taxed differently. They are not taxed as separate entities, but their shareholders are taxed on their pro rata portion of company earnings regardless of whether distributions are made. One dollar of earnings from an S corporation would generate, at a 33 percent rate, $.33 of taxes to its shareholders leaving $.67 available after tax. Many specific requirements must be met to qualify as an S corporation. *See: Joint Ventures, Limited Liability Companies (LLCs), Limited Partnerships, S Corporations, Strategic Partnerships.*

Co-Sale Agreements are clauses usually contained in financing agreements that require management members to share any future sale of their stock with the present investors. Sometimes referred to as tag-along provisions, they are usually entered into at the insistence of the outside investors as a condition of their providing funding.

The purpose of a co-sale agreement is to prevent important management members from selling out (perhaps at a large profit) and leaving the investors "holding the bag." While co-sale agreements do not prevent management shareholders from selling their shares at a profit, they do force them to share the benefits of their sales with the investors by allowing the investors to include their shares in the sale.

In practice, co-sale agreements work like this: Whenever a management shareholder is approached and has the opportunity to sell his shares of company stock, he must notify the investors and tell them the terms that have been proposed. Then the outside investors have an opportunity to sell some of their shares to the purchaser. If the outside investors elect to include some of their shares in the sale, the management shareholder will reduce the number of his shares being sold so that the purchaser acquires the number of shares he originally offered to buy. The number of shares the outside investors are entitled to include is usually a predetermined percentage of the total number of shares being sold. Often, that percentage reflects the relative number of shares held by the investors and the selling management shareholder.

The operation of co-sale agreements raises some interesting securities law questions. For instance, does the participation by the outside investors in the management shareholder's sale of shares create an obligation on the management shareholder to provide more formal disclosure to the buyer of the shares than he would otherwise have had to make? Certainly, it creates an obligation on the part of the participating outside shareholders to be as candid with the buyer as the management shareholder is required to be. Just as certainly, the management shareholder has a separate responsibility to the participating outside shareholders to make full and accurate disclosure to them about the offer and the condition of the company. How to fulfill this obligation can be a troublesome question in a real world where companies have extensive activities and even investors who sit on a company's board of directors may not have a full or accurate understanding of the company's operations.

What happens if the buyer of the shares obtains rights against both the management shareholder and the outside selling shareholders because of an inadvertent misrepresentation or omission made by the management shareholder? Has the management shareholder created additional liabilities for himself to the participating investors by permitting them to participate in the sale? (Probably yes.) Does the management shareholder risk incurring liability as a selling shareholder if the participating shareholders make a misrepresentation that entitles the purchaser to rescind the purchase or obtain damages? (Again, the answer is probably yes.)

Because the use of co-sale agreements raises so many securities questions, which in turn can create liability for management shareholders, co-sale agreements should be avoided whenever possible. When they cannot be avoided, cross-indemnification agreements can be used with them to make each party responsible for any liabilities created by their misrepresentations or failure to comply with applicable securities laws.

Co-sale agreements should be for as short a term as possible and should terminate automatically when the company goes public. Management shareholders can also try to limit co-sale rights by making them nontransferable and requiring participating sellers to bear a share of the cost of consummating a sale. These costs could be significant if the sale requires the preparation of an offering circular or other significant disclosure document.

Whenever possible, management should negotiate a minimum number of shares that it can sell in any twelve-month period without triggering the co-sale rights. After all, the rationale for the co-sale provision is to prevent management from selling out wholesale and leaving the investor with an unmanaged company. Sales of small numbers of shares should not diminish management's interest in the company. Sometimes gifts of shares and uses of the shares to secure legitimate debts can be excluded from a co-sale obligation.

In all events, any sales made under a co-sale agreement, whether the outside investor chooses to include his shares or not, should be made only on the advice and with the assistance of counsel. Otherwise, management and the outside investors these rights are designed to protect may find themselves being exposed to unexpected and unwanted liabilities. *See: Blue Sky Laws, Exits, First Refusal Rights, Reg D, SEC (Securities and Exchange Commission), 10b5, 33 Act.*

CPAs (Certified Public Accountants) are professionals who, by training and certification, are qualified to audit a company's financial statements. These audits can help attract some (but certainly not all) investors and are essential for going public. CPAs can be sole practitioners or members of a larger firm.

Companies that do not have an accountant who is experienced in working with emerging growth companies should consult with an outside accountant to establish company accounting systems that are appropriate to their businesses. Even a company with a good accountant can usually benefit from the counsel of an accounting firm that has experience with growing companies. Such firms can help management decide what types of books and records the company should keep and what types of regular reports management should receive to help it manage its business and attract investment. These firms can also help management design a bookkeeping system that anticipates rapid growth and provides mechanisms to make it easier to manage the problems such growth inevitably brings.

Many accounting firms also help companies prepare projections and draft business plans. Many have valuable contacts in the business community and can provide introductions to potential investors. Some even assist start-up companies on a reduced-fee or delayed-billing basis. A relationship with a good accounting firm can also provide a reference for venture capitalists to consult. *See: Audits, Reports and Records.*

Learning to Count on Your Accountant

If you're on the verge of taking your company public, you'll need to rely heavily on accountants. CPAs can assist in crunching numbers for the prospectus and all related documentation required by the Securities & Exchange Commission. They can also help you evaluate the track records and terms offered by different underwriters, and put you in touch with securities lawyers. And they can establish internal controls and systems to keep your reporting timely and accurate after you've completed your offering, structure compensation packages, and advise you on computerized financial services.

Entrepreneurs "can't go public at a decent price without an opinion from a well-recognized public accounting firm," says William Lerach, partner in the San Diego office of Milberg Weiss Bershad Specthrie & Lerach, a securities law firm. (Over 87 percent of 193 IPOs with share price $5 and above went with a Big

Eight firm, according to a month-long *Venture* study of IPOs in 1985.) Big Eight firms typically subject the financial statements of IPOs to at least three levels of senior partner review—that's usually enough, along with their reputations, to reassure most underwriters and prospective investors, as well as the SEC, which requires disclosure of all materials (including balance sheet and profit and loss statements) relevant to the offering.

Going public begins with audits. The process includes reviewing such internal controls as your cash disbursement and accounts payable and receivable systems, and testing transactions and account balances that are "material" to your company. If you have bought an expensive piece of equipment, for example, an accountant will want to see the purchase order, the canceled check, and the actual machine.

Accountants necessarily are fussy people. Audited financials require them, for instance, to observe inventory firsthand each year. If they can't, CPAs must qualify their opinion of the financial statements when filing with the SEC, which can mandate a delay until reliable inventory records have been established. Accountants recommend that startups considering an IPO have inventories verified at least two years in advance of their target date. Similarly, acquisitions that are considered "material" to a company—for example, anything that cost more than 10 percent of total assets—must be audited separately for at least one year. Without such an audit, filing can be put off for months or years.

The standard registration statement—form S-1, used for offerings of any size, but generally for those exceeding $7.5 million — demands audited balance sheets for the previous two years and audited income statements for the past three fiscal years. Prior audits by another accounting firm must be reviewed for compliance with SEC regulations. If a company hasn't been audited in past years, IPO accountants must reconstruct the financial past as best as they can.

Only rarely is a company preparing to go public so disorganized that an audit is impossible. More often, startups have at that point simply outgrown their record-keeping systems. Typical problems of such companies include unreconciled bank accounts, poor accounts payable systems, and uncollected receivables that haven't been written off. Often, new companies fail to keep close track of inventory values, notes payable, and underlying collateral, sometimes pledging the same assets more than once. On occasion clear records of issued stock and options may not exist.

Accountants can also help you by filing what are known as supplemental schedules—a more detailed balance sheet as well as income statement information—for plants and equipment, land and leasehold improvements, allowances for bad debts, and total depreciation expenses. In the prospectus, CPAs render their opinion, either "clean" or qualified, that no material financial information has been misstated or left out. They must draft and send to underwriters a comfort letter — explaining how charts, graphs, and all statistical data were derived, and giving updated financial information—no more than three days before a prospectus hits the Street.

The entire auditing process takes about three to six months. You can save time if your records are in ace condition. Count on spending $25,000 to $200,000, depending on the complexity of the job: that is, the condition of your records, the nature and size of your business, and the difficulty of reporting details about acquisitions and divestments.

From an article by Michelle Bekey in the April 1986 issue of Venture

Cram Down refers to a negotiation where one party has so much leverage over the other that it is able to dictate deal terms that are extremely favorable to it. Although often civil, the negotiation sessions in a cram down are characterized by the lack of meaningful give-and-take on the substantive issues. They occur most often in situations where one party knows that the other party has no viable alternative to accepting the offered deal. *See: Bridge Loans, Leverage, Negotiation.*

Cumulative Voting refers to a particular method of voting shares of stock that can be provided for in a company's governing documents. It allows a shareholder to cast all of his votes for company directors (determined by multiplying the number of his shares by the number of director positions being filled) for just one director. Cumulative voting can be used to ensure a minority shareholder that he will have a seat on a company's board of directors.

In a normal voting arrangement, a shareholder with 30 percent of the voting stock can never be assured of any representation on a company's board of directors. This is because each director position is voted on separately. As each position is voted on, the 70 percent shareholder can outvote the 30 percent shareholder and, thereby, elect all of the directors.

With cumulative voting, the result is different. Instead of electing each director separately, all the director positions are voted on at once with the top vote-getters taking seats on the board. If three positions are being filled, each shareholder gets three votes for each of his shares. He can vote them in any fashion he wants.

With three positions open, a shareholder with 30 shares gets 90 votes (three times 30 votes), while a shareholder with 70 shares gets 210 votes (three times 70 votes). If the 30 percent shareholder votes all of his 90 votes for one candidate, that candidate is guaranteed to be one of the top three vote-getters because the remaining 210 votes can only give two other candidates more than 90 votes. Since the three candidates receiving the most votes are elected to the board, the 30 percent shareholder is assured of being represented on the board. *See: Common Stock, Control, Management Agreements, Minority Shareholder, Shareholders' Agreements, Voting Agreements, Voting Trusts.*

Cure Periods refer to provisions in agreements that allow a defaulting party to "fix" the cause of a default. In a financing agreement, a cure (or sometimes "grace") period provision might state that if the company fails to perform a required task, such as meeting goals that are a condition of obtaining more funding from the investor, the company will, nonetheless, be given an extra thirty days in which to perform that task before it is held to be in default of the agreement. If the company meets the goal within the cure period, the investor becomes contractually bound to provide the next round of funding. *See: Benchmarks, Default, Stage Financing.*

D

Deal refers to the final agreement between management and an investor for the funding of a company. The terms of the deal are set forth in financing agreements that both sides have reviewed and negotiated carefully. A deal is normally very different from the offer, the counter offer, or the final offer. In some cases, the deal is quite different from what either management or the investor originally envisioned. The time required to complete a venture capital deal can vary from several weeks to several months.

In conversation, entrepreneurs and investors speak of good deals, bad deals, sour deals ("the deal went sour"), sweet deals (a deal that is particularly lucrative), side deals (a secondary deal enabled by the first deal), and raw deals (deals in which one party thinks he has been outmaneuvered). No matter how a deal is described, it involves at least two parties and their attorneys, all of whom may characterize it differently. *See: Closing, Deal Breakers, Deal Flow, Financing Agreements, Negotiation, Structure.*

Deal Breakers are individuals who are so interested in something other than closing a deal that they hinder or stop a financing without good reason. No one wants a deal breaker near an important negotiation.

Deal breakers can be hard to distinguish from friends and counselors who try to help management get a good deal. They come in assorted varieties.

- The *hard-liner* believes that the best way to negotiate is to take firm positions and not discuss the issues. He presents a proposal on a take-it-or-leave-it basis and acts annoyed when a legitimate issue is raised by the other side. The hard-liner's intransigence results in a dead deal even when the parties' respective interests could have resulted in a good deal for both sides. The best deals are usually made between parties who discuss their concerns intelligently and search creatively for common ground on which a deal can be based.

- The *minutiae master* wears everyone out with his obsessive concern for detail. He wants to document every detail regardless of its practical importance to the deal. This sometimes disguises the fact that he does not understand its economics. He is often heard repeating phrases such as "we did it this way on the last deal" or "this is our standard language, we always insist on it."

- The *best dealer* is obsessed with getting the best deal. Instead of working to get the best deal available, he insists on a deal that is so good for him and so bad for the other party that it cannot be made. The best dealer often appears as an adviser to a businessman who is unsure of himself and does not completely understand the economics of the proposed transaction.

- The *last dealer* wants the current deal to be exactly like the last one he worked on. It doesn't matter to him that this deal is different: He understood the last deal and will do everything he can to force this one into a format with which he is familiar. Since his last deal is different from the present deal, the other side will object. If he goes unchecked, the deal will die.

Deal breakers can be hard to distinguish from advisers who have the parties' best interests at heart. This is because their deal breaking is related to some hidden agenda, such as fulfilling their personal idea of what a tough negotiator is or hiding their inexperience with the funding process. By contrast, good negotiators are not constrained by personal agendas that are unrelated to the goals of the negotiation. They are able to keep the goals of their parties clearly in focus throughout the negotiations and work diligently, using all their creativity and experience, to obtain the best deals. For the entrepreneur, distinguishing between an adviser who is a deal breaker and one who is a good negotiator can mean the difference between success and failure. *See: Deal, Deal Flow, Negotiation, Shopping, We Always Do It This Way.*

Deal Flow refers to the never-ending stream of business proposals that come to most venture capitalists for review. It is common for a venture capital firm to receive more than 100 business proposals each month. Therefore, it is not unusual for a venture capitalist to invest in less than 1 percent of the deals arriving at his doorstep.

Deal flow explains why an outstanding business plan is so important. Also, it explains why venture capitalists can often insist on the structure of the deals they will accept. The best way an entrepreneur can address this inflexibility is to approach more than one venture firm at a time. Few venture capitalists will object or lose interest in a company's proposal when an entrepreneur takes this approach. Soliciting more than one venture capitalist can create healthy competition among investors and enhance a company's bargaining position. In the best case, several capitalists will bid against each other to fund an attractive deal. This happened frequently in computer-related financings of the 1980s, resulting in excellent deals for the computer entrepreneurs, and rude awakenings for the investors several years later. This is not to say, however, that companies should shop their business plans indiscriminately to a large number of investors. To do so shows a lack of sophistication on management's part and can discourage interest from investors. *See: Business Plan, Business Plan Format, Shopping, Summary.*

Debentures are one form of corporate note, under which a company borrows money and agrees to repay it with interest. They represent a legitimate alternative for companies to raise funds without selling equity. Many investors fund both debt and equity and use debentures to reflect the debt portion.

Investors sometimes use debentures to increase their return on investment. This happens when they characterize a portion of their equity investment as a debenture while computing the amount of stock they require on their total equity and debenture investment. When this is done, the investor receives money as a debt repayment without reducing his potential return from the stock purchase. If the investment is only moderately successful, the debenture also helps the investor reclaim a portion of his money for investment in another company.

How can characterizing a portion of an investment as a debenture benefit investors at the expense of management? Assume, for example, that an investor agrees to provide $600,000 in return for 30 percent of a company's outstanding stock. The investor wants to pay $100,000 for the stock and $500,000 for a debenture. The debenture proposed will have a term of ten years, and the company will not have to repay any principal or interest until then. In the meantime, if the company generates enough profits to pay off some of the debenture without hurting cash flow, then the company will begin to do so.

The investor's preference for this structure is clear. If he invests all $600,000 in the stock and the company succeeds, his initial investment may pay back $2 million, for example, making his profit $1.4 million. If, instead, he puts $100,000 in the stock and $500,000 in a debenture, his profit will be more than $1.9 million because, in addition to the $2 million, he also gets paid back his $500,000, with interest. In the first case his return on his stock investment is 2.3 to 1; in the second case it is more than 19 to 1!

But does it matter to the company? Should the company begrudge the investor a higher return as long as it does not cost more? Consider the following:

The investor argues that the structure does not hurt the company or management. The company still gets $600,000. If it does well and meets its projections, the company can pay back the debenture early. If the company does not do well enough by the tenth year to pay back the debenture, it probably will not matter because, he says, management will probably have abandoned the project by then anyway. It is a corporate debt, after all, and if the company cannot make the payment, it will not be doing well enough to keep the entrepreneur's loyalty anyway. There's no personal liability (at least, not now), so management should not care.

The proposed structure does allow the company to use the $500,000 without making interest payments during the start-up years of its operations. It may even help the company to borrow other funds as long as the debenture holder's rights are subordinated to another lender's. It will not, however, improve the company's balance sheet to the same extent or give a lender as much comfort as an equity investment will.

The terms of a typical debenture require a company to start repayment after three or four years of operation (if the company is generating enough cash). If the company is expanding at that point, as everyone hopes it will, management may need cash to support larger inventories or more ambitious marketing efforts. Therefore, if management agrees to the investor's proposed structure, the company may incur the expense of further borrowing earlier than it would have had to if the original investment had been for all stock.

Thus, the use of a debenture reduces the value to the company of the venture capitalist's investment. It may not reduce it below what is needed to get the company started, but it does reduce it in a measurable way. As a result, companies should try to structure debentures they issue in ways that reduce and delay their adverse effects. Here are some ways to accomplish this.

- *Make the term as long as possible.* The longer the company has the money to use before it has to repay the loan, the more like equity it is to the company. (This also applies to interest payments and early principal payment required by the terms of the debenture. These principal "prepayments" typically become due when the company exceeds its projected profits.) To the extent possible, these obligations should be delayed even if they are made contingent upon the success of the company's operations.

- *Reduce the portion of the investment made as a debenture and make required prepayments small.* Ideally, any prepayment obligation should be small, start late, and be at management's option. If the investor wants interest on optional prepayments that the company chooses not to make, payment of that interest should not be required until late in the term of the debenture. The financing agreements should make it clear that any failure to make prepayments or interest payments before the end of the term will not give the investor any rights to require earlier payments under the debenture.

- *Persuade the investor to subordinate his debenture to other debt of the company.* This will make it easier for the company to borrow additional cash, which, in turn, makes it easier for the company to succeed. Success of the company, after all, is the primary goal of management and the venture capitalist; without that success the debenture is worthless.

- *Negotiate a right to force the investor to convert the debenture if certain events occur.* For example, if the company meets its performance goals, give management the option to force conversion of the debenture into equity and thereby improve the company's debt-to-equity ratio and make it easier for the company to borrow from outside lenders. Management may choose not to exercise the option if new equity is cheaper than new debt, but the option could prove valuable in the right situation.

You can also try to convince investors to make the company's payments on the debentures contingent on company success and not require an absolute obligation for the company to repay the debenture at the end of ten years. But do not expect an investor to be too sympathetic to this suggestion. Without a definite repayment obligation, the IRS may treat principal repayments under a debenture as dividends to the investor. This means unwanted taxable income to the investor and a reduction in the debenture's after-tax value. As long as the IRS recognizes the debenture as a legitimate debt, repayments of principal create no income and no taxes to the investor.

The use of a long-term debenture does not decrease the risk to the venture capitalist that he will lose all of his money if the company fails. It does, however, increase the size of his reward if the company succeeds. At the same time, the debenture decreases the value of what the company receives from the venture capitalist. This being the case, there is a basis for management to argue that the venture capitalist should be entitled to less stock for his investment when a debenture is included in the funding structure.

Do not confuse debentures with convertible debentures. "Straight" debentures do not give investors any options to buy additional stock. Convertible debentures do. If a venture capitalist requests convertible debentures, be sure the number of shares the company is willing to sell equals the number he buys outright plus the number his convertible debenture entitles him to buy. *See: Convertible Debentures, Convertible Securities, Debt Service, Leverage, Structure, Subordinated Debt.*

Debt Service is the amount of money a borrower must pay to his lender in order to keep his loans out of default. It consists of the interest and principal payments required to pay off the loan.

Debt service payments reduce cash flow, which explains why equity investments, which do not require repayments, are often preferable. Debt service also explains why certain types of venture companies, such as Small Business Investment Companies (SBICs), Minority Enterprise Small Business Investment Companies (MESBICs), and Business Development Companies (BDCs), usually structure their fundings as loans with warrants instead of as straight equity purchases. These types of companies rely on borrowed funds to provide all or most of their capital. By using loans when they invest, these venture firms are able to use the debt service payments from their portfolio companies to repay their loans and stay out of default. *See: BDCs (Business Development Corporations), Cash Flow, Default, Debentures, Leverage, MESBICs (Minority Enterprise Small Business Investment Companies), SBICs (Small Business Investment Companies).*

Default is the failure of one party to fulfill its obligations to another party under an agreement. A company default usually gives substantial rights to the investor. Depending on the nature of the default and terms of the contract, those rights could empower an investor to withhold funding, to take over the company, or to accelerate the company's obligation to pay off debt.

Whenever possible, management should try to limit an investor's default rights to circumstances that involve material defaults so that inconsequential, technical defaults do not cause the company to be penalized. Rights to remedy or "cure" defaults can often be obtained and written into an agreement. These cure rights permit a company to correct defaults and avoid the severe penalties they can involve. *See: Benchmarks, Cure Periods, Projections, Take Away Provisions.*

Demand Rights are contractual agreements that entitle an investor to force a company to register his shares of company stock so that he can sell them to the public. Demand rights are often contrasted with piggyback rights, which allow an investor to include his shares of stock in a public offering that the company voluntarily conducts for its own benefit.

Most venture capitalists require companies to grant them demand rights as a condition to their investing. Demand rights enable the investor to liquidate his investment by forcing the company to register his shares for sale to the public. This registration process, however, is expensive and time-consuming. And a public sale at the wrong time can reduce the future value of a company's shares. Because this can increase a company's cost of raising equity in the future, the number of demand rights granted and the conditions under which they can be exercised are usually heavily negotiated issues. The outcome of those negotiations can seriously affect the value of a funding and the future success of a company. *See: Piggyback Rights, Private Placements, Registration Rights.*

Dilution (Percentage) is a decrease in the percentage of a company's outstanding stock represented by a fixed number of shares. Percentage dilution occurs to existing shareholders whenever a company issues shares of stock to a new shareholder. It results from the increase in the total number of company shares outstanding caused by the sale of new ones. This increase reduces the percentage ownership each share represents in the company. As a result, existing shareholders who do not purchase new shares find themselves owning a smaller percentage of the outstanding equity.

For example, if management owns all 80,000 shares of a company's stock and the company issues 20,000 new shares to another investor, management's percentage ownership in the company will be reduced from 100 percent to 80 percent. Its 80 percent of the stock may be worth more than the 100 percent it owned before the new investor bought 20,000 shares, but, nonetheless, management's stock ownership has been diluted.

Percentage dilution is inevitable in venture capital financings. In fact, few entrepreneurs manage to retain a majority of the stock in their companies by the time they go public. Still, 25 percent of a $50 million company with publicly traded stock is worth a lot more than 100 percent of a privately held company worth $5 million. Not only is it more than twice as many dollars, but it is also in a more liquid form, which itself adds value to the stock.

The most important factor about percentage dilution is how great it is and how much money the company receives for the stock it sells. In general, for a growing company, the longer outside equity financing can be delayed, the less percentage dilution management will suffer. See: *Antidilution Provisions, Dilution (Value), Going Public, Pricing, Restricted Securities.*

Dilution (Value) is an accounting concept. It refers to the difference between what an investor pays for his shares of company stock and their book value immediately after the transaction. Whenever an investor pays more than book value for his shares, he suffers value dilution.

Assume, for example, that an investor buys twenty thousand shares at $10 per share when eighty thousand shares are already outstanding and the book value of the company is $50,000. The investor's $200,000 investment will be added to the $50,000 to increase the company's book value to $250,000. Dividing the company's new book value by the number of outstanding company shares gives the per-share book value. In this case, the $250,000 book value divided by one hundred thousand shares (the investor's twenty thousand plus management's eighty thousand) gives a per-share book value of $2.50. The investor who paid $10 per share suffers a $7.50 per-share value dilution. At the same time, management's shares experience an increase in book value from $.62 per share ($50,000 divided by eighty thousand shares) to $2.50 per share.

Venture investors expect value dilution. They know that book value is only one method of measuring a company's worth and that, in most cases, it is a conservative measure. Most investors are more interested in the fair market value of the shares they purchase and the company's prospects for success. *See: Antidilution Provisions, Dilution (Percentage), ROI (Return on Investment).*

Percentage and Value Dilution Comparison

Management share ownership	80,000
Investor share purchase	20,000
Total shares after purchase	100,000
Investor price per share	$10
Company book value before investment	$50,000
Company book value after investment	$250,000
Company per share book value after investment	$2.50
Percentage dilution of management (100% to 80%)	20%
Per share value dilution of investor ($10.00 to $2.50)	$7.50

Directors' Indemnities are pledges of a company's credit to protect the members of its board of directors against liabilities they might incur when acting on behalf of the company. Most states permit corporations to provide these indemnities for their directors. Usually, the indemnities apply only when the directors are acting in good faith. Most states exclude from protection actions taken by directors that are willfully fraudulent or grossly negligent.

Venture capitalists usually require these indemnities to be included in a company's bylaws before they invest in a company or join its board of directors. A common indemnity provision reads like this:

> *Indemnification of Officers and Directors.* The corporation shall indemnify any current or former director, officer, employee or agent of the corporation, or any persons who are or were serving at its request as a director, officer, employee, trustee or similar functionary of another foreign or domestic corporation, trust, partnership, joint venture, employee benefit plan or other enterprise, against any and all liabilities and expenses actually and necessarily incurred by such person in connection with or resulting from (a) any threatened, pending or complete action, suit or proceeding, whether civil, criminal, administrative, arbitrative or investigative, (b) an appeal in such an action, suit or proceeding, or (c) an inquiry or investigation that could lead to such an action, suit or proceeding, all to the full extent permitted by law. Such indemnification shall not be deemed exclusive of any other rights to which such person may be entitled, under any bylaw, agreement, insurance policy or vote of shareholders, or otherwise.

See: Board of Directors, Board Committees, Bylaws.

Discounted Cash Flow refers to a method of valuing a company that is commonly used by private company investors. Unlike the market valuation method described in the *Pricing* entry, the discounted cash flow method estimates company value without resort to the price-earnings ratios of similar publicly held companies.

The premise of the method is that company value can be estimated by forecasting future performance of the business and measuring the surplus cash flow generated by the company. The surplus cash flows and cash flow shortfalls are discounted back to a present value and added together to arrive at a valuation. The discount factor used is adjusted for the financial risk of investing in the company. The mechanics of the method focuses investors on the internal operations of the company and its future.

Like any other valuation method, the discounted cash flow method has its shortcomings. Since it focuses only on the generation of cash flow, it ignores outside factors that affect company value, such as price-earnings ratios. It also ignores asset values and other internal factors that can reduce or increase company value.

Nonetheless, it is a commonly used method in venture capital financings because it focuses on what the venture investor is actually buying, a piece of the future operations of the company. Its focus on future cash flows also coincides nicely with a critical concern of all venture investors, the company's ability to sustain its future operations through internally generated cash flow.

The discounted cash flow method can be applied in six distinct steps. Since the method is based on forecasts, a good understanding of the business, its market, and its past operations is a must. The steps in the discounted cash flow method are as follows:

- *Develop accurate, debt-free projections of the company's future operations.* This is clearly the critical element in the valuation. The more closely the projections reflect a good understanding of the business and its realistic prospects, the more confident investors will be with the valuation its supports.

- *Quantify positive and negative cash flow in each year of the projections.* The cash flow being measured is the surplus cash generated by the business each year. In years when the company does not generate surplus cash, the cash shortfall is measured. So that borrowings will not distort the valuation, cash flow is calculated as if the company were debt free. In other words, interest charges are backed out of the projections before cash flows are measured.

- *Estimate a terminal value for the last year of the projections.* Since it is impractical to project company operations beyond three to five years in most cases, some assumptions must be made to estimate how much value will be contributed to the company by the cash flows generated after the last year in the projections. Without making such assumptions, the value generated by the discounted cash flow method would approximate the value of the company as if it ceased operations at the end of the projection period. One common and conservative assumption is the perpetuity assumption. This assumption assumes that the cash flow of the last projected year will continue forever and then discounts that cash flow back to the last year of the projections.

- *Determine the discount factor to be applied to the cash flows.* One of the key elements affecting the valuation generated by this method is the discount factor chosen. The larger the factor is, the lower the valuation it will generate. This discount factor should reflect the business and investment risk involved. The less likely the company is to meet its projections, the higher the factor should be. Discount factors used most often are a compromise between the cost of borrowing and the cost of equity investment. If the cost of borrowed money is 10 percent and equity investors want 30 percent for their funds, the discount factor would be somewhere in between.

- *Apply the discount factor to the cash flow surplus and short fall of each year and to the terminal value.* The amount generated by each of these calculations will estimate the present value contribution of each year's future cash flow. Adding these values together estimates the company's present value assuming it is debt free.

- *Subtract present long-term and short-term borrowings from the present value of future cash flows to estimate the company's present value.*

The following table illustrates the computations made in the discounted cash flow method. The table assumes a discount factor of 13 percent and uses the perpetuity assumption to generate a residual value for the cash flows after the fifth year. The numbers contained in the *Discount* column represent the present value of 1.00 discounted back at 13 percent per year.

Year	Cash Flow	Discount	Present Value
1	$ (50,000)	0.885	$ (44,250)
2	10,000	0.783	7,830
3	60,000	0.693	41,580
4	150,000	0.613	91,950
5	310,000	0.543	168,330
Residual value	1,294,846	0.480	621,526
Present value of projected cash flow			886,966
Subtract: Outstanding debt			150,000
Present value			$ 736,966

Using the perpetuity assumption to determine the residual value was done by dividing the fifth year's cash flow ($310,000) by the discount factor (13 percent). This resulting value represents the value of the company at the end of the fifth year and must be further discounted back to present value, as shown in the table.

Since the discounted cash flow method can only estimate value by using agreed-upon assumptions, it is always wise to compare the valuation generated through this method with valuations generated through other methods, such as the market valuation method described in the *Pricing* section of this book. Also, changing the assumptions in the calculations can create large swings in "value." Because of this it is wise to test the assumptions used carefully. *See: Cash Flow, Pricing.*

Downside is the investor's risk that he will lose the money he invests in a company. While the downside in almost every venture investment includes some possibility that the investor will lose all of his money, most investors use the term in a limited sense. They use it to describe a realistic appraisal of the probable risk in the situation.

Investors often talk about the downside in terms of possible scenarios the company's operations might follow. Some try to quantify the likelihood that the company will fail and the amount of money (or percentage of their investment) they will lose if it does. In the final analysis, however, there is usually as much "gut feel" in an investor's estimation of downside as there is hard analysis. For any company, the more likely it is to fail and the more money its investor stands to lose in a failure, the greater its downside and the less likely it is to attract an investor.

Venture investors use a number of deal-structuring devices to reduce their downside risks. Often, they delay parts of their funding obligations and make them contingent upon the companies meeting predetermined benchmarks. This allows an investor to postpone risking some of his money until a company has proven its ability to meet a goal. The later rounds of funding are put in at less risk when the company is more established. Taking collateral and guarantees also reduces the downside by increasing the probability that the investor can salvage something if the company goes under. Preferred stock and debentures do the same thing by giving the investor a preference over common stockholders when a company is liquidated.

Other investor practices also reduce the downside. Investor due diligence not only helps the investor pick good companies but also helps him avoid losers. Board of director seats and required reports from management help investors identify and, hopefully, correct problems early. Puts, buy-sells, redemptions, and registration rights can liquidate an investment before all is lost or help an investor get his money out of a modestly successful company and into something else.

Management can reduce the downside too. When it does, management increases the chance of getting funding at a reasonable price. The best way to reduce the downside is to anticipate strategic and operating problems and address them realistically in the business plan. This won't eliminate the downside entirely, but it will increase the investor's comfort and help management deal better with problems as they arise. Since most of the deal-structuring devices that reduce the investor's downside tend to increase the risks of management shareholders (by delaying needed funding, making it contingent on future events and giving preferences to the investor when the company fails), precautions that reduce everyone's risk (such as good planning) not only help attract new investors but also enhance the value of the management's shareholdings. *See: Business Plan, Business Plan Format, Collateral, Convertible Securities, Co-Sale Agreements, Debentures, Due Diligence, Exits, Liquidity Agreements, Negotiation, Pricing, Puts, Stage Financing, Structure, Upside.*

Due Diligence is the independent investigation of a company, its management team, and its prospects for success by an investor before funding is provided. Due diligence is usually intensive and thorough and often takes months to complete.

Due diligence customarily includes background checks on the management team, independent verifications of statements made in the business plan, and studies of the company's product and market. It includes extensive questioning of management and other company personnel. Most venture capitalists will talk with company suppliers, customers, competitors, and others who know the company and its industry.

Entrepreneurs should conduct due diligence too. They should investigate their industry and their partners thoroughly to gauge their company's prospects and the depth of experience and commitment of each of its principals. Business plans should not be completed without giving careful attention to the assumptions and "facts" that support the company's profits and cash flow projections.

Just as important, entrepreneurs should conduct due diligence investigations about the company's potential investors. Selecting the right investor for a company can mean the difference between success and failure. A disreputable or reluctant investor can slow and even prevent company success. Conversely, an honorable investor can help management by giving it the benefit of his experience with growing companies and his contacts with financial institutions. This can be as valuable as cash.

One way to learn about a particular investor is to ask bankers, lawyers, and accountants about his reputation. If a publicly held venture capital fund is considering investing, a good deal of information about it can be obtained from the Securities and Exchange Commission. If it is privately held, management can usually obtain a copy of the offering circular it used to raise funds by simply asking the investor for one. The National Venture Capital Association, National Association of Small Business Investment Corporations (NASBIC), *The Corporate Finance Sourcebook* and *Pratt's Guide to Venture Capital Sources* by Stanley Pratt can also provide valuable information about the size of a fund and the types of investments it makes.

Once it has begun investigating a company, most venture firms will give an entrepreneur a list of the companies in which it has invested. These companies can provide valuable insights into the operations of the venture firm and its desirability as a business partner. Appropriate questions to ask the founders of these companies are as follows:

- Was the firm easy or difficult to work with?
- Was it prompt in making investment decisions?
- What type of participation in management did it require?
- Are its officers honest and candid?
- Were they reasonable in their negotiations?
- Have they provided services promised to the company?
- Have they helped or hindered company success?
- Are they responsive to company needs?
- How has the firm reacted to company problems?
- Is it flexible?
- Has the firm participated in later rounds of financing?
- Did it help identify further investors?
- Did its performance live up to its promises?

The more specific the questions are, the more valuable will be the information obtained. Questions to and about the venture capital firm are appropriate and demonstrate management's concern for the future. Questions about how long it will take the investor to make a decision and whether it has the funds and freedom to make an investment are particularly appropriate. *See: Audits, Business Plan, Downside, Ethics, Five Factors, NASBIC (National Association of Small Business Investment Companies), National Venture Capital Association, Three Questions, Venture Capitalists.*

E

Earnouts refer to acquisitions or leveraged buyouts (LBOs) in which the purchaser, usually management, finances part of the company's purchase price by borrowing from the seller. In the purest form of the arrangement, the purchaser is required to pay the earnout portion of the purchase price only from the profits of the company. If the company does not earn enough profits under the new owners to pay off the seller, the seller may become entitled to take the company back, receive certain minimum payments, or increase the purchase price. The term earnout is also used to refer to venture capital financings in which a portion of the funding is provided by a loan that is repaid only from company profits. *See: Earnups, LBO (Leveraged Buyout).*

Earnups are arrangements whereby an investor acquires most of a company's capital stock but gives management the opportunity to increase its stock ownership by managing the company successfully. Usually, management operates the company under a contract that allows it to control the operations of the company as long as the company meets specified goals. Earnups are less a financing device than they are a technique for attracting good people to manage a company. Sometimes earnups are used in a leveraged buyout (LBO) by the outside investor to entice existing management to remain with the company. If management can keep the company profitable and meet its goals, it often can earn a substantial equity position in the company. Earnups assign little value to management's role in putting together the funding used to purchase the company. Instead, they reward management for making the company succeed after the funding. *See: Earnouts, Golden Handcuffs, LBO (Leveraged Buyout), Management Agreements, Vesting Schedules.*

EGCs (Emerging Growth Companies) are what venture capitalists are eager to add to their investment portfolios. They are companies that promise to grow fast and create a healthy return on investment for their investors. This is customarily achieved when the company, now just "emerging" as an attractive investment, does well enough to support a public offering or attract a corporate purchaser in three to eight years. EGCs are usually in industries whose stocks tend to sell at high multiples of company earnings; thus, it takes fewer dollars of earnings to support a high stock price when the investor later sells.

High-tech companies are not necessarily emerging growth companies. While it is true that high-tech companies have attracted a lot of venture capital investment, it is not because they are high tech. They have received funding because they tend to be in industries that support high price-earnings ratios.

EGCs include any company that presents good potential for rapid and sustained growth (growth in excess of the industry average or the gross national product). Low- or no-tech companies with the potential for rapid and sustained growth are being funded. The venture capitalist's primary concern is final return on investment when the company stock attains liquidity, not the glamour of high tech. *See: High Tech, Price-Earnings Ratio, ROI (Return on Investment).*

83(b) Election is an option employee shareholders have under Section 83(b) of the Internal Revenue Code. It entitles them to choose when they will be taxed on shares they purchase from their employer when their shares are not fully vested.

Anyone who receives stock in connection with the performance of services for a company should know about Section 83 of the Internal Revenue Code. Unless an 83(b) election is made, Section 83 can require the shareholder to pay taxes at ordinary income tax rates when the restrictions on his stock lapse. The tax is computed on the difference between the value of the stock when the restrictions lapse and the price paid for the shares. This tax must be paid even if the shareholder cannot sell his stock to generate cash.

Section 83(b) entitles the shareholder to make an election within thirty days after he purchases the shares to prevent this unwanted attribution of income. The election (basically, filing the proper form) causes the shareholder to be taxed at the time of the purchase, instead of the date of vesting. This earlier tax is based on the difference between the purchase price of their shares and the value those shares would have had when they were purchased if they had been fully vested.

Why would someone choose to be taxed earlier instead of later? Because, as is often the case in early stage companies, the initial low purchase price for the shares may equal the actual market value of those shares at that time. When this is the case, making an 83(b) election creates no tax liability at the time of purchase and prevents tax liability from arising when the restrictions lapse on the stock. This effectively defers the employee's tax obligation until he sells the stock.

Even the employee who purchases the stock for less than its value may choose to make the election. If the employee believes the stock will increase dramatically in value, he may prefer to be taxed now on a relatively small amount rather than risk being taxed on an amount which is much greater when the stock fully vests.

The chart below, which assumes that the shares were sold at a discount to the employee, illustrates the workings of Section 83(b).

	No Election	Election
Price of shares	$10,000	$10,000
Share value at purchase	$12,000	$12,000
Value taxed on sale	none	$2,000
Share value when restrictions lapse	$90,000	$90,000
Value taxed when restrictions lapse	$80,000	none
Value taxed when shares sold for $100,000	$10,000	$88,000

As the chart illustrates, failure to make an 83(b) election can have disastrous effects. If, as everyone involved hopes, the company increases in value during the vesting period, the shareholder who failed to make the election will have to pay taxes on the difference between the increased value of the shares on the date they vest and the amount he paid for them. At the same time, the shares are likely to be illiquid (unsalable) because of restrictions that apply to unregistered securities. As a result, the shareholder may owe the federal government a substantial tax payment (caused by his failure to make an 83(b) election) without having the means to pay it. In the example, failure to elect to pay taxes on a $2,000 gain results in the employee owing taxes on $80,000 of "paper income" when the restrictions lapse.

The provisions of Section 83 are complex and cannot be completely explored here. They apply in situations when a casual observer would not think they should. As a result, any person who receives or purchases securities that are subject to vesting or other similar restrictive provisions should consult with a qualified attorney or accountant to determine whether the filing of an 83(b) election is appropriate. *See: Restricted Securities, Vesting Schedules.*

Employment Contracts are agreements between a company and its employees that set forth the terms of their tenure. They are used for a variety of purposes, including attracting key people to join a company by guaranteeing their salaries or describing their benefits. They can also be used to define job duties or to bind employees to secrecy and noncompetition agreements. Employment contracts can provide protections against arbitrary firings. If properly written, they can even help companies avoid expensive fights over trade secret infringement claims made by former employers of newly hired company personnel.

Employment contracts with key employees are important to many investors. Young companies usually depend more on the talents of a small group of people than do their larger, more established competitors. Because of this, most investors require assurances that a company's key people will remain after funding. They want to know that the people they evaluated will stay around to run the company with their money. At the same time, entrepreneurs often want protection against being fired when new investors are brought in. It is no surprise, then, that an important negotiation in many venture financings deals with who will enter into employment contracts and what the terms of those contracts will be.

Employment contracts do not always make sense for a company, however. As a general rule, employment contracts should be avoided unless they serve a specific company purpose. Giving an employee a contract that guarantees his employment for a period of time does not further company interests unless it is necessary to secure an important benefit for the company, such as convincing the employee to take the job. Because of the personal-service nature of employment, employment contracts are usually ineffective at forcing an employee to stay with a company. They are even less effective at keeping an employee interested in doing a good job. At the same time, however, employment contracts can cause management to retain an employee longer than it wants or to pay a departing employee a premium to leave.

Investors' preferences for contracts with management does not mean they like rich employment contracts. They expect entrepreneurs to sacrifice present earnings for the prospects of long-term capital appreciation. Managements that crave large salaries and elaborate executive benefits can scare away venture capitalists. Contracts that ensure management employment for too long or in circumstances that could jeopardize a shareholder's investment also cool investor enthusiasm.

Venture investors want the freedom to remove management if it proves to be ineffective. At the same time, managements want some security against arbitrary firings. Employment contracts are designed to reconcile these different points of view. *See: Compensation and Bonus Plans, Confidentiality Agreements, Golden Handcuffs, Noncompete Agreements, Vesting Schedules.*

Entrepreneur is someone who accepts the many risks inherent in operating an enterprise in pursuit of profit. The term can apply to anyone who forsakes the relative security of a job for the challenge of building a successful company. Most entrepreneurs invest great amounts of time and effort, at considerable sacrifice to themselves and their families, for the privilege of starting their own businesses and being their own bosses. Entrepreneurs come from all walks of life and have different degrees of experience and ability.

What do venture capitalists look for in an entrepreneur? What type of people do they like to invest in? Here are a few characteristics venture capitalists like to find in an entrepreneur.

- *Achievement.* Investors look to past experiences as a prime indicator of an entrepreneur's prospects for success. Someone who has been successful in the past is more likely to be successful in the future. Obviously, the best achievement an entrepreneur can have is to have started a business in the same industry. Next to that, success and advancement in a large company are preferred.

- *Knowledge.* Knowledge of the industry and where a new product will fit is essential. An accurate study of the industry may give an entrepreneur this knowledge, but actual experience in it is a real plus. Knowledge about working with people and the ability to put together a good management team is important.

- *Energy.* A venture capitalist must be convinced of an entrepreneur's ability and willingness to work hard to make the company a success. A tenacious entrepreneur with enthusiasm for his company is a must. Surveys show that entrepreneurs work long hours.

- *Intelligence.* What an investor looks for here is rationality, insight, and creativity. Advanced degrees from universities are nice and may evidence intelligence, but what a venture capitalist really wants is an entrepreneur who can analyze a complex problem, understand it, and arrive quickly at an appropriate solution.
- *Flexibility.* No one wants to invest in a blockhead! A flexible entrepreneur is one who can adjust his approach to meet unexpected problems. He is one who can accept criticism and advice from others, including his investors. Most important of all is the entrepreneur's ability to learn from his mistakes and grow with the increasing demands of his expanding company.
- *Management ability.* A successful company's management will be faced with personnel and management problems that would stretch the patience and creativity of the best of managers. A good manager must be able to work with and motivate his people. He must also keep a tight rein on cash flow, cash control, manufacturing, and sales.
- *Integrity.* Investors want an entrepreneur who is honest and open with them and with himself. This integrity includes an honest appraisal by the entrepreneur of his strengths and weaknesses as well as a realistic appraisal of his product and its prospects for success in the marketplace.

All entrepreneurs have faults. The more of these "ideal" characteristics an entrepreneur has, however, the more likely it is that his company will get funded. Investors consider these characteristics carefully when they evaluate business proposals. *See: Commitment, Due Diligence, Ethics, Five Factors, Management Team.*

Entrepreneurs Are Different

Harvard Business School research (summarized by John Kao in the *American Banker*, March 16, 1984) finds no single, unitary, entrepreneurial psychology. Rather, that research has identified some recurrent traits or themes among entrepreneurs:

- A high tolerance for ambiguity
- High levels of creativity
- An ability to tolerate paradox in one's personal style, for example to be highly intuitive and at the same time attentive to detail in a highly disciplined fashion.

That research sounds intriguing, but we should be cautious in shouting from the roof tops whatever new findings are unearthed in studies focusing entirely on entrepreneurs.

One midwestern entrepreneur club, for example, polled its membership and found very little except that they had strong mothers. This complements a *Venture* survey of its readers (November 1985) that found entrepreneurs describe some kind of childhood deprivation—emotional, physical, or financial—in the father-child relationship.

According to a Gallup poll summarized by Ellen Graham in the *Wall Street Journal* (May 20, 1985), entrepreneurs are often loners or misfits. They tend not to be joiners or team players and are far more likely to have been fired from jobs than top executives. These findings are especially trustworthy because they represent the results of three samples comparing the opinions of entrepreneurs in young, rapidly expanding companies with those of both businessmen in more well established companies with slower growth rates and executives in Fortune 500 posts.

Joseph Mancuso, president of the Center for Entrepreneurial Management in New York, says that entrepreneurs are misfits, out of step. "Corporate executives get to the top by offending the least number of people, while the entrepreneur gets to the top by stepping over those in his way."

One consistent finding in both academic studies and public opinion polls is that entrepreneurs are not high rollers, but tend to be moderate risk-takers. And a Gallup poll found that "protecting the company from risks" was their most important job characteristic. Even their investments are not any riskier than those of non-entrepreneurs.

Denial of the possibility of failure, eternal optimism in the face of both success and failure, feeling exhilarated by the stress and challenge of launching an enterprise—these characteristics all sound like a description of some kind of inspirational or religious experience. A *Venture* survey (January 1986) confirms the religious strain among entrepreneurs, a finding that of 1512 respondents, nearly seven out of ten (69%) from both smaller and larger businesses believe that the strength they gain from religion helps them cope better with business-related problems. The specific characteristics of a particular religion may be less important than one of the chief functions of religion generally, which is to assert a faith in optimism in the face of life's uncertainties.

From this perspective, entrepreneurs may be misfits only in the sense that their optimistic faith is more resilient and harder edged than that shown by other contemporaries.

From a speech by John Crothers Pollock, Ph.D., chairman,
New World Decisions, Ltd., delivered to a Venture/Adweek seminar
for advertising professionals

Equity is ownership. It is what is sold to investors to get them to fund a company and what is retained by the entrepreneur to reflect the value of what he has created. It represents the value of a company as a going concern. Equity is the most permanent form of investment in a company. It does not require repayment and so does not deplete company cash, as debt repayments do.

Usually, equity takes the form of stock ownership and is different from rights a person may have under a note, debenture, or other debt instrument. Convertible debentures have characteristics of both debt and equity. They are treated as debt until the holder elects to convert them. Then they lose their debt characteristics and become equity.

Equity has an element of magic. Some of the most outrageous, unlikely, seemingly ridiculous business ventures have been undertaken with the object of creating equity. The pursuit of equity is as deeply a part of the American entrepreneur as is the pursuit of happiness. *See: Cash Flow, Common Stock, Convertible Debentures, Convertible Preferred Stock, Convertible Securities, Debentures, Equity Penalties, Preferred Stock.*

Equity Kickers refer to stock or options to purchase stock that are given by a company to a lender as an inducement to lend money to the company. *See: Options, Warrants.*

Equity Penalties are agreements, usually contained in written contracts, that increase an investor's percentage of ownership upon the occurrence of a specified event, such as the failure of the firm to reach a sales level on a given date. By increasing the investor's share of the company, equity penalties decrease the share of other investors, including management.

Be wary of equity penalties. They include any arrangement that results in management's stock ownership percentage decreasing if the company fails to achieve its goals. Equity penalties can be in the form of investor options, specialized antidilution protections for outside investors, or restrictions that prevent management shares from vesting.

Equity penalties are often legitimately included in venture fundings. They are used to allocate risk among the parties. Sometimes, however, equity penalties sneak into a deal late in negotiations as a "sweetener" for the investor. The first hint that an investor wants this type of "sweetener" often comes when the investor suggests to management that if the company does not meet the projections in its business plan, then his investment will not be a good one.

To get the funding, management probably made a good sales pitch to the investor. In the course of its many discussions, management probably reassured the investor several times that the company's projections were reasonable and attainable. Now the investor suggests that if the company does not meet its projections, his return on investment will not be high enough to justify his investment. The fair thing to do, he says, would be to increase his equity percentage if the company fails to meet its projections.

At this point, most entrepreneurs get heartburn. They have spent a lot of time with the investor and have become accustomed to thinking of the deal as done. If they refuse this "reasonable" request, they might lose their funding. The temptation to concede is great. But is the request reasonable? Should management concede the investor's request? Usually not.

Most investors know how difficult it is to accurately project results and do not really expect management to concede this issue. After all, the value of management's investment also diminishes if company projections are not met. And one reason the investor is getting so much equity for his money in the first place is because of the risky nature of the investment.

When an investor insists on equity penalties and management has neither the time nor inclination to look for other investors, it should nonetheless try to get the investor to require "extra" equity only if the company does not attain 70 percent or 80 percent of projected results. Management should also try to work in a time cushion. If the projections show the company reaching a certain result on January 1, for example, management should try to get until April 1 to reach 80 percent of the projections.

Finally, management can suggest that if it makes sense for the investor's percentage to increase if the company fails to make its projections, that it also makes sense for his percentage to decrease if the company exceeds them. An investor will often concede the fairness of this proposal and console himself with his original offer for a fixed percentage of the company. *See: Benchmarks, Business Plan, Earnouts, Earnups, Negotiation, Projections, Take Away Provisions, Vesting Schedules.*

Ethics are critically important in venture capital transactions. The relationship of entrepreneur and venture investor is so intertwined that when one acts unfairly, the other almost always suffers. Even when the parties carefully document their agreements, either party can be ruined by the unethical behavior of the other.

Investors recognize the need to deal only with people they can trust and direct a good bit of their due diligence work toward determining whether entrepreneurs are honest and trustworthy. Entrepreneurs should be just as careful to examine their investors' reputations.

An unfair or reluctant investor can cause real problems for a company. If he fails to provide funding or delays or reduces the funding he agreed to provide, he can steal a company's promise and starve it for cash. This cash shortage can delay expansions and product developments. It can cause the collapse of a company that is not yet profitable. At the very least, it distracts management from the day-to-day management of the company and forces it to deal, instead, with the cash crisis created by the investor.

What is more, this same cash crisis often prevents the company from enforcing its contracts against its investor. Even if the company's contracts require the investor to fund, the company may be unable to force the investor to live up to his bargain. This is because the investor's unwillingness to fund takes away the two assets management needs most to force him to do so: money and time. In many cases, the company simply cannot afford to spend its money or time trying to force an unwilling investor to fund. Even if it could, the actions required to do so would be a serious drain on the company and might frighten other investors away. After all, how many investors want to put money into a company that is suing its prior investor?

At the same time, the investor may frustrate management further with new demands that make it difficult for the company to obtain money from other sources. As a result, just when management needs to concentrate its efforts on building its company, it is forced, instead, to find cash and deal with an uncooperative investor who has acquired significant rights in the company. The best way to avoid these problems is to be careful when selecting investors, to investigate their reputations, and to try, when possible, to deal only with people who are trustworthy. *See: Adventure Capitalists, Cash Flow, Due Diligence, Stage Financing, Unlocking Provisions.*

Executive Summary. *See: Summary.*

Exits are how venture capitalists liquidate their investments and take their profits. The three most common exits are public offerings of company stock, sales of company stock or assets to a corporation, and liquidity agreements. The exit formula, or how the entrepreneur envisions the investor will eventually liquidate his investment, is a critical section of the business plan. An entrepreneur must demonstrate that he understands and anticipates the investor's exit. He must be ready to answer the investor when he asks, "How and when do I get out?" The best answer is, "In five years via a public offering or sale to a corporate buyer, at five times your original investment." The time period method and multiple can be changed to suit the deal. *See: Business Plan Format, Buy-Sell Agreements, Cashing Out (or In), Co-Sale Agreements, Downside, Going Public, IPOs (Initial Public Offerings), Liquidity Agreements, Puts.*

F

Factoring is a form of receivables financing. The factor (or lender) pays the company a discounted portion of the company's receivables and then collects those receivables directly from customers as they become due.

Factoring differs in popularity by industry. It is perhaps most widely used in the garment industry, in which orders are shipped well before the season when they are to be sold, but vendors cannot (or do not) pay for the merchandise until it is sold. A factor will buy the invoices from the manufacturer at a discount. The manufacturer receives the factor's money and shows the invoice as paid. The factor collects the full face value of the invoice and accepts the risk of doubtful accounts. *See: Collateral, Inventory Financing, Receivables Financing.*

Financing Agreements are the final contracts that document the outcome of the negotiations between the entrepreneur and the investor. In a typical financing of debt and equity, the financing agreements might consist of a stock purchase agreement, a registration rights agreement, a shareholders' agreement, a loan agreement, a note or debenture, and the stock certificates issued to the investor.

Financing agreements are usually long and involved. Their provisions identify the amount of funding and the conditions under which funds are released. They spell out the types of securities the investor receives and any special shareholder rights he has negotiated for. Financing agreements also contain provisions that govern the ongoing relationship of the investor and management. Many contain penalties if the company's results do not meet specified expectations.

Because of their breadth and complexity and the far-reaching effects their provisions can have on a company and its continued viability, financing agreements should be reviewed carefully. Each provision should be considered for its long-term impact as well as its short-term benefits. *See: Affirmative Covenants, Boilerplate, Closing, Convertible Securities, Debentures, Investment Reps, K.I.S.S., Lawyers, Letters of Intent, Management Agreements, Promissory Notes, Negative Covenants, Negotiation, Operating Covenants, Registration Rights, Reps and Warranties, Shareholders' Agreements, Structure.*

First Refusal Rights (Company) are agreements, usually in writing, that give investors the opportunities but not the obligations to participate in future company financings. Except when they are granted to avoid giving an investor another, more onerous right, first refusal rights should generally be avoided. They do not guarantee a company any funding and often make it more difficult to find new investors.

As a practical matter, however, many venture investors insist on some sort of first refusal right as a condition to their investing. Some use first refusal rights like options to secure the opportunity to purchase more shares in the future. Some use them for antidilution protection. The first refusal rights enable them to retain and increase their ownership in a company by purchasing shares at then current rates. Others use them to exercise control over who the company's other investors will be.

First refusal rights are usually structured in one of two ways. One variation allows the company to negotiate with others for needed capital, but only if it gives the first investor a right of "first refusal" to provide the desired financing on the same terms management negotiates with its other investor. Under this variation, management can discuss but cannot close a funding with another investor until the first investor declines to take the deal. The other type of first refusal right requires the company to present the first investor with the opportunity to invest on terms suggested by the company. If the first investor does not make the investment, the company is then free to negotiate with others to provide the funding on terms no more favorable to the new investor than those presented to the first investor.

Both variations impair a company's ability to raise money. The first form can make it very difficult because most potential investors are reluctant to negotiate with managements when they know the deals they make can be taken away from them by other investors. In fact, many investors will not even talk with a company's management unless it has the ability to close the deal it is offering.

The second variation also chills a company's ability to obtain financing because it requires the company to construct an investment proposal for the first investor before it has had an opportunity to shop around to see what the best available deal is. It requires the company to begin looking for money earlier because the first investor must be given time to evaluate the investment proposal. If the first investor declines to make the requested investment, the company is still restricted in how much equity it can sell to obtain the money needed.

In general, first refusal rights should be avoided and investors should be comforted, when possible, with company exhortations of loyalty and the reality that money is hard to find. If the right of first refusal is insisted upon, the second form of right of first refusal is generally preferable. Under that scenario, once the company has presented its investment proposal to the first investor, it is free to go and negotiate with others. Unlike the first variation, the company will be able to tell those other investors that it can close the deal it is negotiating.

Sometimes an investor will accept the addition of a twist to the second type of first refusal right that makes it more palatable to management. This requires the first investor who rejects the company's offer to either make a binding offer of his own to fund the company or release it completely from the right of first refusal. If the investor waives the first refusal right, the company is free to negotiate with others. Even if the investor does not waive his refusal rights, the company can proceed to try to negotiate a better deal with outside investors. If it cannot make a better deal, it can still accept the first investor's offer. *See: Antidilution Provisions, First Refusal Rights (Shareholder), Options, Preemptive Rights, Warrants.*

First Refusal Rights (Shareholder) refers to rights of first refusal given by company management to the company's investor. They are common in venture financings. The purpose of these first refusal rights is to protect the investor when a key management member decides to cash out his investment.

Often used with co-sale provisions, the first refusal right enables the investor to prevent an unwanted party from becoming his partner by letting the investor purchase shares management proposes to sell. Most first refusal provisions entitle both the investor and the company to buy the shares. If the shares are for sale at an attractive price, the investor and remaining management may choose for the company to buy the shares so that they can be used to attract a qualified person to replace the selling manager.

Sometimes management can negotiate for first refusal rights from the investor in exchange for the first refusal rights given by management. When these rights are received, they are usually exercisable by both company and management. First refusal rights should terminate with a public offering or sale of the company. *See: Buy-Sell Agreements, Co-Sale Agreements, First Refusal Rights (Company).*

Five Factors refer to criteria venture capitalists use when evaluating a company. Knowing something about these criteria can improve an entrepreneur's odds of getting funded by helping him focus his business plan on the factors that matter most to investors.

Stanley E. Pratt, former publisher of the *Venture Capital Journal* and noted venture capital authority, identifies five principal factors venture capitalists look for in a company. Those factors are: management, management, management, market niche, and product or service.

Mr. Pratt recommends this list to make a point. Many entrepreneurs overemphasize their product or service when making a presentation to an investor. They fail to realize that investors tend to be more interested in a company's ability to build a business than they are in its particular product. Most experienced venture investors have seen plenty of good, even spectacular, product ideas fail. At the same time, most investors have seen companies succeed in ways they did not anticipate when funding was solicited. It is the management team, therefore, that many investors consider to be the single most important ingredient for a successful company.

Another prominent venture capitalist, Frederick R. Adler, identifies five different factors his company uses when investigating a company. The potential for large, long-term profits is the first factor. To fulfill the requirement a company must be able to forecast significant, profitable growth over an extended period of time.

The second criterion relates to whether the company has the right technology at the right time. A product that is too revolutionary or not revolutionary enough might not qualify. Technology that is easily replicated would fail too, especially if large competitors exist with superior channels of distribution. The third criterion is potential for high profits. High profits improve cash flow and make it easier for companies to grow. Companies in markets that are intensely price-competitive might not qualify under this criterion unless their products can be produced for significantly less than their competitors' products. This criterion can be hard to meet when a market does not already exist for the company's product. When this is the case, investors cannot be certain of profit margins or even of the company's ability to build a profitable market.

Management is the fourth criterion. All investors look for companies with complete and well-rounded management teams. Investors like managers who are not only competent, but who are flexible and open-minded. The characteristics Adler and Company looks for when evaluating a manager are: judgment, aggressiveness, sincerity, experience, and charisma. The fifth, and last, factor considered is what value the investor can add to the company. Money is important, but the investment potential of a company is enhanced if the investor can offer the company something more in the way of experience or contacts. *See: Business Plan, Business Plan Format, Commitment, Entrepreneur, Management Team, Value Added, Windows.*

Venture Capitalists Bet on Management

A survey of the investment criteria used by 100 professional venture capital firms revealed that the entrepreneurs' "capability for sustained intense effort" was the most important of the 24 factors listed in the survey questionnaire. The survey, conducted by New York University's Center for Entrepreneurial Studies, asked 100 venture capital firms to rank on a scale of 1 to 4 the factors they considered before investing in venture proposals. Ranking just after "capability for sustained intense effort" was "thorough familiarity with the market targeted by the venture" and "demonstrated leadership ability in the past." At the bottom of the ranking were "the venture will create a new market" and "I will not participate in later rounds of investment."

Here is a list of the 10 criteria most frequently rated essential by the survey respondents.

Item	Percent
Capable of sustained intense effort	64
Thoroughly familiar with market	62
At least ten times return in 5 to 10 years	50
Demonstrated leadership in the past	50
Evaluates and reacts to risk well	48
Investment can be made liquid	44
Significant market growth	43
Track record relevant to venture	37
Articulates venture well	31
Proprietary protection	29

The failure to satisfy these criteria in most cases means the venture is "disqualified" for investment.

From an article in the July 1985 issue of Venture's Capital Club Monthly

Flip refers to the practice of selling a company or an investment made in a company soon after the purchase to make a quick gain. They are most often seen in leveraged buyouts (LBOs) or other whole company acquisitions where circumstances permit a bargain purchase. When this is so, the opportunity sometimes exists for the purchaser to resell or "flip" the company in a short period of time to another buyer at a higher price.

A flip can be costly to management in an LBO if the investor uses debentures or preferred stock as a primary investment vehicle but takes his equity interest in common stock. This is because management typically acquires the smaller equity interest in the transaction and the investor's structure requires the debenture or preferred stock to be paid out before moneys are paid to shareholders. Until the company's value exceeds the debt by a significant margin, management's share in the equity will be less than anticipated.

In an LBO that cost $5.5 million, for example, management might own 20 percent of the company's common stock to the investor's 80 percent interest. If the investor structured $5 million of his investment in debentures, a flip of the company in six months for $10 million will pay out $5 million to the investor on the debenture and another $4 million on his common stock. Even though the company nearly doubled in value, management will receive only 20 percent of $5 million or $1 million instead of 20 percent of the total $10 million purchase price. The investor, by contrast, makes a neat $4 million profit on a $5 million investment made for six months.

This problem can be effectively addressed in the financing agreements. If it is not, it can create a powerful incentive for the investor to flip the company for a quick profit in circumstances where management might be better served by growing the company for a longer period of time to a higher value. *See: LBO (Leveraged Buyout).*

Forecasts. *See: Projections.*

Franchising refers to a form of licensing that businesses use to expand and generate revenue. It is generally characterized by the license from a franchisor to a franchisee of a trademark and system of doing business. In return for the license, the franchisee pays the franchisor an up-front fee, which is often substantial, and agrees to pay the franchisor a percentage of sales or some other royalty in the future.

For the right kind of business, franchising can reduce the need for venture capital by enabling the franchisor to obtain capital from its franchisees. In most franchising arrangements, the cost of expanding to a new business unit is borne by the franchisee. The franchisor advises the franchisee in the best methods of establishing his unit of the business and charges him a fee to cover the cost of providing that advice and to make a profit. After the business begins operating, the franchisee pays the franchisor a percentage of sales or other agreed-upon royalty.

Franchising does not usually replace the need for outside equity. Capital is almost always needed to develop the franchise system and protect the trademark. In many cases, franchising is pursued only after the company has owned and operated a few successful units of its business itself. This operation takes time and usually requires considerable capital to fund. Traditional venture capital sources are receptive to funding businesses that plan to grow through franchising.

Establishing a franchise program requires the preparation of an extensive franchise disclosure document, which provides information about the franchisor and the franchise program. Careful compliance with both federal and state franchise and business opportunity laws is a must. Failure to comply with all of the requirements can result in significant liability to a company and its managers. *See: Licensing, Trademarks.*

G

Geography refers to a simple fact: Companies that are conveniently located to their markets and to investors' headquarters are more likely to get funded than those that are not.

Venture capital funds invest more than money in companies. They invest time and expertise as well. An investor's experience and business contacts can be valuable to a company. As a consequence, venture firms operate most efficiently when the companies they invest in are located relatively close to their headquarters. The next best case for a venture investor is to have his investments located in clusters that allow him to monitor several investments on one trip. (One venture capital investor we know of invested only in cities from which a round trip could be completed in one day.)

When selecting venture capital firms to approach, geography suggests that a company should stay as close to home as possible. When approaching a firm located a long distance away, management should be sensitive to the fact that the venture investor may want to make a joint investment with a local firm or one that has a portfolio of investments near the company's headquarters. Companies located away from suppliers and customers should be careful to describe to investors how they plan to overcome the inconveniences this causes. The business plan is the best way to address these problems and their solutions. *See:*

Networking, Syndications, Value Added. But see also: Shopping, Specialty Funds.

Going Public refers to a company's first sale of its securities (usually common stock) to the general population of equity investors. It is accomplished by registering those securities with the federal Securities and Exchange Commission (SEC) and state securities commissions and then selling them to the general public. The sale itself is usually conducted by a professional underwriter. Going public is a goal of many companies that seek venture capital. It enables them to raise money from the public and creates a market for subsequent sales of their stock. It also creates an easily ascertainable market value for shares.

Many entrepreneurs think longingly about going public. They see it as a confirmation of the success they have worked long and hard to attain. They believe that the money and other benefits generated by a public offering are worth the effort and expense required to complete it.

But going public is not always the right decision and does not always indicate success. Seeking funds from private investors or from traditional lending sources may make more sense.

Determining whether going public makes sense requires consideration of a number of factors including timing, company history, prospects for future growth of the company and the industry, and management's personality. The advantages and disadvantages of going public should be weighed carefully before a decision is made to seek funds in the public markets. Among the advantages management should consider are the following:

- Lower cost of capital
- Capital for continued growth

- Increased shareholder liquidity
- Future financings
- Enhanced ability to expand
- Improved company image

Lower cost of capital. Going public is often triggered by management's belief that it can raise more money and get a better price for its stock by selling to the public than to a venture capitalist or other private investor. When this is true, a public offering can raise money at less cost and with less dilution of management's shareholdings.

Going public becomes cost effective for most companies when they finally meet the profile required to attract institutional investors to the offering. While this profile varies according to market conditions, it generally requires sustained growth and profitability over a significant period of time, a company valuation of at least $10 million, prospects for continued growth at a rate greater than the industry average, and an offering of at least 100,000 shares at prices of $10 or more. When a company matures to the point of meeting this profile, its ability to attract institutional investors often boosts the price of its stock high enough to make going public the most economical way to raise capital.

Capital for continued growth. Perhaps the most obvious benefit of going public is the proceeds (cash) of the offering. These moneys can be used for a variety of company purposes as long as they are disclosed in the company's offering documents. Typical uses are to increase working capital, to acquire new divisions or technologies, to increase marketing efforts, to pay for research or plant modernization, or to repay debt.

Increased shareholder liquidity. Going public makes it easier for company shareholders to sell their shares by creating a public market for the company's stock. Shareholders who register their shares in the company's offering hold freely tradeable shares once the offering is completed. Even the shares that are not registered in the offering become more liquid. Because of the offering and the periodic reporting requirements it imposes on the company, shareholders often qualify after a prescribed period of time to sell limited numbers of their shares under Rule 144. If they want to sell more shares than Rule 144 permits, they can benefit from easier and less expensive methods available for registering their shares that are available to public companies. *See: Restricted Securities.*

Future financings. Most public offerings raise a significant amount of equity capital and thus dramatically improve the company's net worth and debt-to-equity ratio. This, in turn, makes it easier for a company to borrow money from commercial lenders at competitive interest rates. Also, an existing public market for the company's stock makes it easier for the company to sell additional equity. If the company's stock does well (that is, increases in price), the company can offer for sale additional shares of stock or a new class of stock.

Enhanced ability to expand. The market created by going public makes it easier for a company to expand through acquisitions and mergers. Because registered shares can be converted into cash, a public company can often use its stock instead of cash to acquire a company or other valuable property. With the proper deal structure, the use of shares instead of cash can ease the immediate tax burden of the seller caused by the sale of his company and, thereby, make the acquisition easier and less expensive to close. Liquid stock also makes a company's stock and option plans more valuable and, thereby, makes it easier for a company to attract and retain the key employees it needs to help it grow.

Improved company image. Going public, with all the financial disclosure and investor relations planning it requires, usually attracts the attention of the business and financial press. Free publicity, coupled with the perception that going public is a significant milestone of success, enhances a company's image.

This improved image can make it easier for management to deal with suppliers and customers. Many privately held companies that compete with public ones find their customers and suppliers reluctant to deal with them on equal terms because of their lack of operating history and the confidentiality of their financial data. Going public can erase this distinction and make it possible for the company to compete more effectively.

The advantages of going public can be substantial, but they can be outweighed by the disadvantages. It depends on management's goals and the circumstances of the company. Among the disadvantages that should always be considered are the following:

- Expense
- Loss of confidentiality
- Periodic reporting
- Reduced control
- Shareholder pressure
- Restrictions on stock sales

Expense. Going public is expensive. The underwriter's discounts alone can amount to as much as 6 to 10 percent of the total proceeds of the public offering. (In a $5 million offering, this can be as much as $500,000.) Other expenses, which include the underwriter's out-of-pocket expenses (typically not included in the underwriter's discount), filing fees, transfer agent fee, legal fees, printing fees, and accounting fees can add another $200,000 to $400,000 to a company's cost of going public. Most of these expenses must be paid at the closing of the offering.

Going public also subjects a company to annual and quarterly financial reporting requirements imposed by the SEC. Complying with these requirements increases the company's costs of doing business. Time and money are required to generate the information necessary for these reports.

Loss of confidentiality. Going public forces a company to prepare and distribute to potential investors a complete description of the company, its history, its strengths, its weaknesses, and its future plans. Detailed disclosures of financial information are required. Information about the shareholdings and compensation arrangements of management and holders of large blocks of stock is made public. All of this information must be updated and supplemented in reports required by the SEC. Once information is filed, it can be obtained by competitors, employees, customers, suppliers, union organizers, and others.

Periodic reporting. Going public subjects a company to a number of periodic reporting requirements with the SEC. These requirements include annual and quarterly financial reports (on Forms 10-K and 10-Q) as well as prompt reporting of material events that affect the company (on Form 8-K). For most companies, these and other reporting requirements, which force the company to maintain audited financial statements, increase the company's cost of doing business by imposing more stringent accounting practices and by making additional demands on management's time.

Reduced control. A public offering can reduce management's control over a company if outsiders obtain enough stock to elect a majority of the company's board of directors. Whenever this is true, outside shareholders can remove members of the management team. (This is not a risk inherent only in public offerings, however. Any sale of voting stock to raise money reduces the percentage ownership of management. Sales of a majority of the company's voting stock to a few private investors, in fact, may make management's ability to retain control less certain than a public offering, which distributes those same shares to a greater number of investors. The larger number of shareholders in a publicly held company can make concerted action by the outsiders more difficult.) Public companies are more susceptible to unfriendly takeover because their shares are easy to accumulate.

Shareholder pressure. Even managements that retain voting control over their companies find that going public subjects them to pressures that can affect the way they run their businesses. Many entrepreneurs find that shareholder expectations and the quarterly reporting requirements of the SEC combine to create significant pressure on a company to continually improve its performance on a quarter-by-quarter basis. Failure to meet these shareholder expectations can cause the market value of the company's stock to decline, making it more expensive for the company to raise money or acquire other companies using its stock. This pressure to meet short-term goals can tempt management to forgo necessary long-term planning when it includes present-day sacrifices that will be reflected in the company's quarterly reports.

Restrictions on stock sales. Only those shares registered and sold in the offering become freely tradeable. Nonregistered shares remain subject to the same trading restrictions as they had before the offering. Moreover, the SEC imposes additional restrictions on the ability of major shareholders and company insiders to sell company stock.

The factors that should be considered when a first public offering is contemplated are numerous and complex. This discussion does not cover them all. Entrepreneurs should consult with their accountants, attorneys, investment bankers, and other advisers before taking their companies public. *See: Control, Investment Bankers, IPOs (Initial Public Offerings), Penny Stock, Private Placements, Public Offering, Restricted Securities, Unit Offerings.*

The Cost of Going Public

Just what entrepreneurs pay to go public is determined by their industry group, the size of the offering, the underwriter that supports them, the quality of their company, and general market conditions. Businesses with a high degree of risk and not much of a track record—including blind pools, which are investment vehicles, not operating companies—may never find a welcome at the top underwriters for their IPOs or hope for a share price above a few dollars and a total offering exceeding $5 million. Such companies shell out at least 10 percent to 15 percent of their proceeds, a portion of their total expenses, to their underwriting troupe. By contrast, older companies with solid operating histories and good prospects for growth can easily sign on with national underwriters, for whose services they pay only 5 percent to 8 percent of their total offering.

How are the costs apportioned? In firm commitment deals, a part of the proceeds goes to the managing underwriter and the syndicate of other brokerages that sign up to sell a portion of an IPO. Whereas the underwriting group must purchase a stipulated number of shares at a discount to the offering price, the selling group has no such obligation. Its compensation is a discount on the shares it sold. Known as the gross spread, this portion of the expenses includes management and underwriting fees and selling concessions—discounts at which shares are allocated to the underwriting group, including individual salespeople—and can range from 5 percent to 15 percent of the total offering.

Other costs of going public are printing and engraving expenses (some $155,000) for preliminary and final prospectuses and legal and filing fees ($50,000 to $350,000), which may include blue-sky registration of the offering in those states where the securities will be sold. Accounting fees run $25,000 to $200,000, depending on the complexity of the audit.

But less obvious costs lurk in many smaller deals. Some underwriters charge a C expense allowance — compensation for, say, office and administrative outlays—that ranges from 1 percent to 4 percent of the total proceeds. Once in a while, firms affix investment banking consulting fees of $24,000 to $48,000 for "general financial matters." Underwriters often pick up more of a company's stock at a discount to the market price by taking warrants.

Even among similar companies the dollar cost of going public varies tremendously. While quality companies can usually find major investment banking firms that charge comparatively lower fees for taking them public, less proven companies end up with small underwriters that cost more on a percentage basis.

From an article by David P. Sutton and
Tom Post in the April 1986 issue of Venture

Golden Handcuffs refers to the combination of rewards and penalties given to key company employees that compensates them so generously for staying and punishes them so severely for leaving that it would be absurd for them to quit the company.

There are two ways to keep valuable people with a company. One is to reward them if they stay. The other is to penalize them if they leave. Many companies combine both approaches by mixing generous economic incentives with noncompete agreements and vesting schedules. If the combination of these incentives and disincentives is effective, they can act as golden handcuffs that prevent the employee from leaving. They do so by raising the employee's expectations of wealth so high that he cannot meet those expectations with another employer, particularly when he considers the restrictions and penalties caused by his leaving. *See: Compensation and Bonus Plans, Employment Contracts, ISOs (Incentive Stock Options), Noncompete Agreements, Phantom Stock Plans, Vesting Agreements.*

Golden Rule differs from the one taught in the Bible. In venture capital, the golden rule is "He who has the gold makes the rules." Many venture capitalists live by this axiom. Since they are providing the cash, they expect to lay down the terms of the funding. *See: Deal, Deal Flow, Leverage, Negotiation, Structure, We Always Do It This Way.*

H

High Tech is a glamorous phrase used to describe any endeavor that involves the application of sophisticated technology. Many people think of venture capitalists as people who fund high-tech companies. The fact is, however, that most venture investors are more interested in return on investment than in the glamour of sophisticated technology. Many do invest in high-tech companies, but only when those companies are also emerging growth companies that promise rapid growth and a healthy return to the investor. *See: Emerging Growth Companies.*

I

Incubators refer to centers that assist entrepreneurs in getting businesses started. They are called incubators because they are designed to help an entrepreneur hatch his idea into a thriving business. Unlike technology development centers, incubators do not restrict their assistance to companies that use advanced technology. They accept high-tech, low-tech, and no-tech companies as participants.

There are a number of incubators throughout the country that offer entrepreneurs a variety of services. There are privately run incubators and incubators that are associated with universities, government agencies, and regional development authorities. The services they provide include inexpensive facilities; free or reduced-cost consulting services from accountants, lawyers, or business consultants; assistance in obtaining government grants and identifying sources of capital; and assistance in marketing and public relations. Entrepreneurs can identify incubators in their locale by contacting their local chamber of commerce, by reading local business publications, or by inquiring of their accountant, banker, or lawyer.

Entrepreneurs should take care to evaluate a center before joining one. The number, quality, and costs of services provided vary from center to center. It is appropriate, when considering an incubator, to meet with and question the center's director about the services available and the qualifications of the persons providing them. It is also helpful to speak with entrepreneurs who are working with the incubator and (even more helpful) with those who have left it.

Incubators can provide valuable services, but beware of "incubator syndrome." The services incubators provide can sometimes sound so good and complete that they lull unprepared businessmen into making the entrepreneurial jump too soon or into relying too much on the center. Joining an incubator is no substitute for entrepreneurial initiative, training, or self-evaluation. Entrepreneurs must remember when joining a center that their personal efforts and resourcefulness are the keys to making their businesses succeed. An entrepreneur with incubator syndrome permits his initiative and judgment to be replaced by those of the consultants who provide assistance at the center. Even if those consultants are superbly skilled and dedicated, they cannot replace the entrepreneur or make his business succeed. Incubator syndrome can be deadly to a new business. *See: Commitment, Entrepreneur, Technology Development Centers.*

U.S. Incubators

Small business incubators are facilities that support new and small firms by providing affordable space, shared office services and management assistance.

Business incubators organized to nurture such enterprises bring under a single roof a number of new and emerging businesses. The period spent in the incubator gives entrepreneurs time to develop management skills which are essential for the successful transition of a start-up to an ongoing, viable small business. The experience, skills, business contacts and access to capital gained while a tenant resides in an incubator helps a firm avert the failure that befalls the vast majority of small businesses within their first few years.

Private incubators run by venture and seed capital investment groups, or by large corporations and real estate development partnerships, usually are concerned with high economic reward for investment in tenant firms and added value through development of commercial and industrial real estate. Such private groups also generally are concerned with new technology applications and other technology transfer.

A third category of incubator operators include universities, which share some of the same concerns as public and private operators. Universities also are concerned with faculty research in connection with incubators, faculty consulting and, for some universities, the opportunity to invest in incubator firms.

From an article in the December 1985
issue of Venture's Capital Club Monthly

Integration refers to the combining of two or more securities offerings under the rules of the federal Securities and Exchange Commission (SEC). When integration occurs, it can cause serious problems for an issuing company and its management.

This is because the federal securities rules treat the combined offerings as one and require that all of the securities sold in both offerings be registered for sale to the public or qualify under a single exemption from registration. If a company conducts two or more offerings (i.e., closes two venture fundings or a private placement and a venture funding), they may be integrated if they are not sufficiently distinct and separate in the eyes of the SEC. This integration can void the registration exemptions that were relied upon even if the company intended for the offerings to be distinct and separate. If the exemptions are voided, the company and management may become subject to significant liability.

Potential integrations of previous offerings with a company's present efforts to raise capital can also delay its ability to raise money without a public offering. Because of this, it is important to determine what constitutes an offering whenever securities are sold.

Factors that the SEC considers when determining whether two or more offerings will be integrated into one include

- Whether they are part of a single plan of financing.
- Whether they involve the issuance of the same class of security.
- Whether they are made at or about the same time.
- Whether the same type of consideration is received for the security.
- Whether the offerings are made for the same general purpose.

There are certain "safe harbors" that can be relied upon to avoid integration when a company is careful. These safe harbors should be taken advantage of whenever possible. If the requirements are met, they can prevent integrations and the liabilities they create. In any event, experienced legal counsel should be retained whenever company securities are sold. It can guide the company safely through the many peculiarities (including avoiding integration) contained in the complex federal and state securities laws. *See: Private Placements, Reg D, Restricted Securities, Safe Harbors, SEC (Securities and Exchange Commission), 33 Act.*

Inventory Financing refers to loans that are collateralized by a company's product before the product is sold, that is, while it is still in inventory. Inventory financing is often contrasted with receivables financing or factoring, when the company's accounts receivables are used to obtain funding. *See: Factoring, Receivables Financing.*

Investment Bankers are financial institutions and individuals who assist companies in raising capital, often through a private placement or public offering of company stock.

Sometimes companies use investment bankers to help identify available financing options or obtain introductions to venture capitalists. Because their business is raising money for companies, investment bankers can help a company analyze its funding needs and identify the most likely or appropriate types of sources for obtaining the money.

This is not to say, however, that any investment banker always can sell any company's business plan to investors. Investment bankers who are experienced with the company's industry and the type of financing it needs often can be helpful in packaging and introducing a business plan or offering circular. If they are unfamiliar with the company's industry or the type of financing being sought, investment bankers may actually hinder a company's financing efforts.

Some venture capitalists believe investment bankers are unnecessary, even disruptive, to a venture funding. They prefer, instead, to deal with an entrepreneur without the intercession of an investment banker. Some entrepreneurs share this view and look to investment bankers only when they prepare to take their companies public. Then, an investment banker's ability to underwrite (or sell) the company's stock can make its services indispensable. Choosing the best investment banker to underwrite a company's initial public offering is an important part of conducting a successful public offering. *See: Going Public, IPOs (Initial Public Offerings), Stage Financing, Underwriters.*

Investment Memorandums are writings that commit an investor to acquire company securities and describe the terms of the purchase. People often use the terms "letters of intent," "commitment letters," and "investment memorandums" interchangeably to refer to short letters of understanding that precede formal financing documentation. *See: Commitment Letters, Letters of Intent.*

Investment Reps are written representations (reps) of the conditions under which an investor has purchased company securities. They customarily appear in financing agreements or in separate "subscription agreements."

Investment reps help complete a funding quickly and cheaply. They do so by giving management the information it needs to obtain an exemption from the expensive and time-consuming registration requirements of the federal and state securities laws. Investment reps should always be required when restricted securities are sold outside a public offering. Used in connection with a proper exemption from registration under applicable securities laws, these representations help protect a company and management from serious securities liabilities. Some common investment reps acknowledge that the investor

- Has purchased the company's shares for investment only and not with a view of reselling them.
- Has made such independent investigation of the company as he has deemed necessary or advisable.
- Has been given free access to company information.
- Is sufficiently sophisticated about investments to judge the merits of investing in the company or has hired someone who is so sophisticated.
- Meets certain minimum wealth or accreditation standards.

- Will not sell the shares purchased without first complying with applicable securities laws in a manner acceptable to company counsel.

See: Blue Sky Laws, Investors, Legend Stock, Private Placements, Reg D, Restricted Securities, 33 Act.

Investors are those individuals and firms who supply money to companies in return for the prospect of capital appreciation. Federal and state securities laws restrict the number and type of investors to whom a company can sell its securities without conducting an expensive and time-consuming registered public offering. Unless the number and nature of the investors qualify the company for an exemption, the company's securities cannot be sold without a registration.

The exemptions most commonly used when a venture capitalist is the investor rely on the venture capitalist qualifying as an "accredited investor" under the securities acts. These accredited investors are persons or entities that are recognized by the statutes as having sufficient wealth, sophistication (or access to sophisticated advice), and access to company information to fend for themselves when examining and investing in a privately held company.

Often, sales to these accredited investors can be made without having to prepare an elaborate private offering circular. By contrast, most of the exemptions that permit private companies to sell their securities to investors who are not accredited require the preparation of an offering circular and close attention to the number of investors solicited, their states of residence, and various state "blue sky" limitations on the number of investors who may reside in each state.

Whoever the investors are, company management should be careful to conduct its stock offering in a manner that complies with all the rules of an exemption from the registration requirements of the federal and state securities laws. Overlooking a single detail can create significant liability for the issuing company and its management.

Whenever an exemption requires a company's investors to qualify as accredited, management should investigate the credentials of the investors to determine whether they meet all of the requirements. The financing agreements should also contain representations from the investors that they are accredited, that they have had adequate access to the company and its management, and that they are capable of bearing the loss should the investment fail.

Elsewhere in this book, we have discussed the value of dealing with good investors, and the negative consequences of dealing with poor ones. Being accredited does not mean an investor is good or ethical. It means simply that he has sufficient wealth and sophistication to fend for himself. Generally, he is someone who has enough other investments that losing his money on one deal will not break him. It is not true, from an entrepreneur's point of view, that money from anyone is better than no money at all. Entrepreneurs should be careful to whom they sell their securities. *See: Blue Sky Laws, Ethics, Investment Reps, Private Placements, Reg D, 33 Act.*

IPOs (Initial Public Offerings) refer to the first registered offering of company securities to the general population of equity investors. They are registered with the Securities and Exchange Commission (SEC) and with the securities commissions of the states in which the company's securities will be offered and sold. The registration of an IPO requires the preparation of a detailed offering memorandum (usually on SEC Form S-1), which contains an extensive description of the company, its reasons for conducting an offering, a description of the securities being sold, an analysis of the risks inherent in investing in the company, and a description of how the company will use the proceeds of the offering. Disclosures regarding the stockholding and compensation arrangements of management and persons with significant stockholdings in the company are also required. Detailed audited financial statements must be provided as well.

Conducting an initial public offering is a painstaking and time-consuming project that requires extensive due diligence by the company's counsel, accountants, and underwriters, and a serious time commitment by management before, during, and after the offering. The offering process usually takes at least three to six months to complete. Typically, these months of preparation include an extensive review of company documents, the preparation of audited financial statements, numerous due diligence meetings between company personnel and the company's advisers, and several drafting sessions (often referred to as "all hands meetings") for the offering memorandum. The preparation also includes filings and discussions with the SEC and with state securities commissions to secure proper registration for the offering, and a "road show" during which the underwriter and company officials take their offer "on the road" to sell the company's securities.

Although IPO schedules vary widely from company to company and are sometimes compacted or expanded to respond to the perceptions of the company's underwriter as to the best time to sell the company's stock, a representative IPO schedule might look something like this:

IPO Schedule

Day 1   Organizational all hands meeting to set schedule and assign responsibilities.

Day 2   Begin due diligence interviews and documents review. Distribute officers and directors questionnaires. Begin selection of transfer agent, printer, and others. Begin preparation of offering circular by company counsel and required financial statements by the company's outside accountants.

Day 30   Distribute first draft of offering circular.

Day 40   First all hands drafting session to review and revise offering circular. Second draft is recirculated ten days later.

Day 60   Second all hands drafting session.

Day 70   Final all hands drafting session to make any final revisions and sign offering circular.

Day 75   File offering circular with the SEC. Issue press release.

Day 85   Begin road show to sell securities. Proceed with state securities registrations.

Day 110   Receive comment letter from the SEC. Prepare response or amendment to offering circular, as appropriate.

Day 120   Determine offering price. Complete state securities filings. File amendment to offering circular, if necessary.

Day 135   Effective date, offering commences.

Day 140   Closing. Company issues securities. Offering proceeds transfer to the company.

Of course, the schedule only outlines some of the major undertakings involved in an initial public offering. The process also involves directors' meetings, extensive due diligence meetings, and the negotiation and execution of contracts with underwriters and others. Often, the process includes the preparation and adoption of employee stock incentive plans or substantial corporate "cleanup" to get the company's books, records, and systems into proper order to become public. *See: Blue Sky Laws, Going Public, Penny Stock, Private Placements, Public Offering, SEC (Securities and Exchange Commission), 33 Act.*

ISOs (Incentive Stock Options) are rights to purchase company securities, usually common stock, which are issued to company employees and others the company wants to hire. ISOs are designed to attract new employees and motivate existing employees. They do this by giving the employee the right to purchase company shares in the future at present-day prices. If the company is successful, and its stock increases in value, the employee can purchase shares of company stock in the future at a price far below the then fair market value of the shares. By creating this potential "windfall," the incentive stock option motivates the employee to work hard to make the company succeed.

ISOs are issued under guidelines adopted by the company's board of directors. These guidelines are commonly referred to as plans.

Federal tax laws recognize two types of ISO plans: qualified stock option plans and nonqualified stock option plans. Preferential tax treatment is given to the holders of options issued under qualified plans. The preference is that there is no realization of income for federal income tax purposes when the option is issued by the company or exercised by the holder.

Employees who hold nonqualified stock options realize income, at ordinary income tax rates, when they exercise their options if the fair market value of the shares purchased exceeds the price they paid for the shares under their option. If the fair market value of the shares is significantly greater than the option exercise price, the employee's tax obligation when he exercises the option can be substantial. Since the employee's profits in the stock may not be liquid (i.e., the stock may be restricted or the market for the stock may be limited), he may have to pay those taxes from his other resources.

By contrast, qualified stock option holders incur no federal tax obligation until they later sell their stock at a profit. No income is realized when the option is issued or exercised. When the stock is later sold, the gain realized is taxed at capital gains rates. (Although current capital gains rates are only modestly different from ordinary income rates, the distinction between ordinary income and capital gains rates could become greater in the future. The capital gains rates have changed frequently in the past, and they have been significantly lower than ordinary income rates in the past. If those rates are reduced in the future, the difference between paying taxes at ordinary income rates when a nonqualified option is exercised and being able to defer those taxes on a qualified option until the stock is sold and then only pay lower capital gains rates will make qualified options even more attractive.)

Securing the benefits of qualification with the IRS requires careful planning and close attention to detail. Qualified options may be issued only under a plan that meets the requirements set out by the IRS. These include having the plan approved by the company's shareholders within twelve months after it is adopted by the company's board of directors. Qualified plans must also identify the types of employees who may receive options and the total number of shares that may be subject to options issued under the plan. Each option may have a term of no more than ten years and must be issued within ten years after the date the plan is adopted. Options may be issued only to employees. Except in certain limited circumstances, employees must exercise their options while they are employed by the company or within three months thereafter.

Further, qualified options may not be transferred except on death and their exercise price must be at least as great as the fair market value of the underlying stock at the time the option is issued. For any employee who holds 10 percent or more of the company's stock, the exercise price must be at least 110 percent of the fair market value of the company's stock when the option is issued, and the option term cannot exceed five years. The total fair market value of stock subject to qualified options that can vest in one employee in one year cannot exceed $100,000. If less than the total $100,000 in value is not used in a given year, however, a portion of the unused part may be exercised in later years.

Plan administrators (usually management) must be careful when they accept notes in lieu of cash payment when a qualified option is exercised. The notes must be full-recourse and must bear interest at least equal to minimum rates established by the IRS. If they do not, the IRS-imputed interest rules will apply. This will require the employee to pay tax on the imputed interest and may, because imputed interest is not included in the option exercise price, cause the latter to fall below fair market value. If it does, the option will not be treated as qualified.

Any incentive stock option plan that does not meet all of the requirements of a qualified stock plan is treated by the IRS as nonqualified. This means the employees will not receive the tax advantages of holding qualified options. However, they also will not be subject to the $100,000 value limitation or to the requirement that they be employees. Nor must the term of their options be tied to employment. Also, below-market interest rate loans used to exercise options will not have a disqualifying effect. If the employee is sufficiently wealthy to pay the taxes, or if the term of the option is long enough to permit him to exercise the option after the company's and his stock becomes tradeable in the public market, the nonqualified stock option may still create a viable incentive for the employee.

Nonqualified options issued to employees also entitle the issuing company to deduct against its income tax obligations an amount equal to the compensation income attributed to the employee upon the exercise of the option. The amount of this deduction is the same as the amount of income attributed and taxed to the employee because of his exercise of the option, the difference between the option exercise price and the fair market value of the shares purchased. To be certain of obtaining the deduction, the company should be sure to withhold the proper amount from the employee's income.

The use of options should be considered carefully so they can be tailored to fit the employee's and the company's needs. Qualified stock options can be used to advantage in most situations and can benefit the employee by giving him the opportunity to share in the future appreciation of the company's stock without adverse tax consequences. To qualify the options the employee receives, however, the company and its management must be careful to structure the option plan to meet all of the IRS's requirements. This usually means engaging a qualified professional to establish and administer the plan.

Also, certain individuals, particularly those who are attempting to shelter income from federal taxation, must be careful to consider the alternative minimum tax (AMT) consequences of obtaining rights under a qualified plan. The difference between the holder's exercise price for the shares in a qualified plan and the fair market value of those shares when he exercises the option is a tax preference item that may become subject to the AMT. The application of AMT rules can make qualified options less attractive to these individuals. Those persons with AMT concerns should consult their tax adviser before accepting qualified stock options. *See: Board Committees, Compensation and Bonus Plans, Golden Handcuffs, Junior Common Stock, Options, Phantom Stock Plans, Warrants.*

J

Joint Ventures refer to business projects undertaken co-operatively by two or more parties where each contributes different skills and resources and shares in the results of the endeavor. Unlike a financing, where one party's contribution is limited to money, joint ventures usually include active participation by all joint venturers. For example, one party might contribute technology and product development expertise while the other manages product manufacturing and marketing and provides the financing to get the product to market.

Joint ventures can be structured as contractual arrangements or can appear as specialized partnerships. They can even appear as corporations with special contractual arrangements among the shareholders. Extensive negotiation to determine the precise roles of the joint venturers is commonplace. More often than not a joint venture succeeds because the contributions of each party complement one another and because the relationship of the joint venturers has been thoroughly considered and documented. *See: Licensing, Off Balance Sheet Financing.*

Junior Common Stock is a class of common stock established by a company's articles of incorporation and action of its board of directors that entitles its holders to lesser rights than the company's regular common stock does. Typically, junior common stock is given much weaker voting, dividend, and liquidation rights than the company's regular common stock, often equal to only one-tenth of those conferred by the latter. Usually, junior common stock becomes convertible share for share into regular common stock upon the company attaining certain predefined goals. Failure to reach those goals cancels the convertibility feature.

Junior common stock is seldom used today. Several years ago, however, it was a common mechanism to grant additional share rights to management as an incentive for outstanding performance. The reduced rights of the junior common stock (or sometimes options to acquire junior common stock) allowed holders to contend that the shares were worth less than their regular common stock counterparts. This, arguably, allowed management to purchase these shares at prices considerably below the market value of the company's regular common stock without having the IRS contend that they were purchasing the junior common stock at below its market value. As a consequence, the argument followed, the IRS would not require the holder to pay taxes on the differences.

By making the junior common stock convertible share for share at a later date, management could eventually trade in its less valuable junior common stock for the company's regular common stock. In order to create an incentive for management and to prevent the IRS from claiming that the convertibility of the junior stock was so certain that the shares should be valued at the higher regular common stock value when they were purchased (and the holder should pay taxes on the difference between what he paid and the fair market value of what he bought), the event that permitted management to convert its junior common stock shares was usually a future performance goal that would be significant for the company and difficult for management to attain.

It was a nice mechanism to reward management for outstanding performance. Unfortunately, the utility of junior common stock decreased dramatically in the 1980s when the Financial Accounting Standards Board announced that in accounting for junior stock transactions accountants must include as compensation paid to the management shareholder by the company an amount equal to the difference between what that holder paid for his junior stock and the value of that stock at the time such conversion became reasonably certain. This would create an expense on the books of the company granting the junior stock rights when it became apparent that it would meet the conversion goals.

Ironically, even though this accounting treatment does not affect the underlying value of the company, by reducing earnings for accounting purposes it can have an adverse effect on the company's valuation in the marketplace since these valuations are often premised, in part at least, on some multiple of the company's earnings. This lower company valuation can in turn reduce the market price of the company's shares and, consequently, make it more difficult for the company to raise money by selling its shares at full value. As a result, junior stock is used infrequently these days as an incentive for outstanding performance. *See: Common Stock, Dilution, Earnups, Golden Handcuffs, ISOs (Incentive Stock Options).*

K

Key Man Insurance is life insurance purchased by a company or investor on the life of an important member of a company's management team. It insures the life of a man who is "key" to making the company a success. Many investors insist on key man insurance as a condition of financing.

K.I.S.S. is short for "Keep It Simple, Stupid!" This may not be artfully phrased, but it is an important principle to keep in mind when negotiating a financing package.

There are many factors that complicate a venture capital funding. Many of those complications are necessary to ensure the best deal to the company. Others, such as registration requirements, are usually imposed by the investor. Nonetheless, management should always be wary of the tendency to overcomplicate matters.

In general, the simpler a company's relationship with its investor the better. Remember, management has to run the company after it gets funded. The less time it has to spend figuring out the twists and complications of the company's deal with its investor, the more time it will have for the productive work of making the company a success. *See: Financing Agreements, Structure.*

L

Lawyers are individuals who have graduated from a law school and passed a bar examination in the state in which they practice. That said, know there are lawyers who understand corporate finance and venture capital financings, and those who do not.

A lawyer who knows corporate finance can be a real help to a company's financing efforts. One who does not know cannot help, and probably will be expensive and distracting. The easiest way to determine whether a lawyer understands financings is to interview him and ask him about his experience.

Venture capitalists almost always use lawyers to prepare and even negotiate their financing agreements. Nonetheless, some venture investors discourage entrepreneurs from employing counsel to represent them in negotiating financing terms and finalizing documents. Others encourage entrepreneurs to keep things simple and hire a lawyer only after the deal has been agreed to, and to limit the lawyer's function to that of reviewing the financing agreements prepared by the investor's lawyers.

The theory these investors espouse is that while they need lawyers to protect themselves from making bad deals and taking unnecessary risks, entrepreneurs need none. But does it really make sense that a venture capitalist who has completed dozens of financings needs a lawyer while an entrepreneur who is new to the whole venture financing process does not? Of course not.

The investor who advises the entrepreneur not to seek professional advice usually does so from personal motives. Certainly, the deal will go easier and better for the investor if the entrepreneur forgoes the advice of counsel and negotiates from a position of inexperience.

The negotiation and documentation of a venture capital financing involve a number of issues of importance to the entrepreneur. Many of these issues are ones that are apparent only to a person experienced in corporate finance who understands the legal and practical implications of the way these issues are resolved. In general, it is wise to enlist the aid of counsel before the terms of the financing are fixed. If a letter of intent or investment memorandum precedes the formal financing agreements, it is best to secure counsel before the letter of intent is signed. *See: Letters of Intent, Negotiation, Structure.*

LBO (Leveraged Buyout) refers to the purchase of a company that uses borrowed money for a substantial portion of the purchase price. If the purchasers are management, the acquisition is sometimes called a "management buyout" or a "management leveraged buyout."

The phrase usually refers to a purchase of a company by its management using moneys borrowed from the seller or a third-party lender for part of the purchase price. The remainder of the purchase price usually comes directly from management and outside investors, often venture capitalists.

Three factors generally are considered essential to conducting a successful LBO: (1) the ability to borrow significant sums (leverage) against the company's assets; (2) the ability to retain or attract a strong management team; and (3) the potential for each participant's (including management's) investment to increase substantially in value. The ability of a company to support significant leverage depends upon whether it can service the principal and interest payment obligations that accompany that leverage. This, in turn, requires a selling company that is capable of generating large sums of cash on a regular basis or that has substantial assets that can be sold to pay off the debt. This usually means a company with a history of operations sufficient to support the borrowing required to fund the deal.

Attracting a strong management team usually means that the division or company being purchased has a strong management team in place that requires few or no changes to make it complete. It is, after all, the investor's and lender's confidence in management's ability to run the company profitably and to expand its operations that makes the buyout possible. Attracting and keeping good management also means cutting them in for a significant portion of the deal. In other words, management usually acquires a healthy percentage of the company's equity. This motivates them to stay with the company and make it grow.

The potential for increase in value of the company's stock comes not only from the ability of strong management to build on an existing base of business but also on the very fact of leverage. The heavy borrowing undertaken to complete a buyout is customarily made directly by the company. This borrowing, because it is large in comparison to the value of the assets of the company, decreases the "value" of the company's stock, enabling management and the outside investors to acquire it at lower prices that reflect the company's value as reduced by the leverage. The leverage results in the common stock having a "value" that is low in comparison to the underlying market value of the company's assets and its historical level of earnings. As the company's debt is paid off, the value of its stock increases, creating wealth for the investors. (It also helps if the underlying assets of the company were significantly depreciated when purchased so that they appear at low book values on the company's financial statements.)

As might be expected, sophisticated cash flow analysis is essential to structuring a successful LBO. Failure to properly project the company's ability to service the debt placed on the company can doom a buyout to failure. This, coupled with the number of parties typically involved in a buyout and the variety and complexity of the financial structures needed to accommodate the divergent interests of the parties involved, almost always requires the involvement of experienced professionals. These include LBO specialists, investment bankers, accountants, and lawyers.

LBOs, when led by existing company management, often involve sensitive negotiations with the company's board and shareholders. These negotiations can be difficult because company management must weigh the risk to its job security created by suggesting an LBO against the necessity of conducting those conversations to determine whether the buyout is possible. Price negotiations can be particularly sensitive since management, not the parent company, is often better equipped to evaluate the company, and management has an incentive to keep the price low. These conflicts can make negotiations intricate and sometimes require the use of an intermediary in the initial stages. *See: Debt Service, Earnouts, Earnups, Flip, Leverage.*

Lead Investor is the company's primary provider of capital. When more than one investor participates in a company's financing, the one who puts together the syndicate of investors who provide the company's funding is referred to as the lead investor. Often, the lead investor serves as the syndicate's representative on the company's board of directors.

Sometimes, however, all or most of the investors in a syndicate will want to be represented on a company's board of directors. When this is the case, it is often because the syndicate members have different motivations for investing and do not feel comfortable having their interests represented by the lead investor. Sometimes the request for more than one seat on the board springs from a lack of confidence in the lead investor or a fund's need to comply with its own organizational requirements.

Whatever the reason, management should resist attempts to place too many members of a single syndicate on its board of directors. With divergent motivations, too many venture board members can create a serious distraction to the business of running a company. More people add more experience to a board, but too many people in any decision-making group make decision making more difficult. Too many directors, particularly if a large number represent outside investors, can make decision making difficult. *See: Board of Directors, Control, Syndications.*

Legend Stock refers to a certificate of equity ownership that carries a description, usually on its face or back, of the restrictions imposed upon the ability of the holder to sell or otherwise transfer its ownership. Most legend stock carries one section identifying the restrictions imposed by state law and another identifying those imposed by federal law. If the holder of the stock has entered into a shareholders' agreement or agreed to some other restriction on his ability to own or resell his securities, these will also typically appear on his stock certificate.

The purpose of legending stock certificates is to alert potential purchasers to the restrictions imposed upon the stock. The absence of restrictive language on a share certificate, however, does not necessarily mean that the stock is freely tradeable and unrestricted. The legends may have been left off by accident. If they were, the purchaser may acquire fewer share rights than he anticipated unless he investigates to determine what restrictions apply. *See: Restricted Securities, Shareholders' Agreements, Vesting Schedules, Voting Agreements.*

Letter Agreements are binding contracts that appear in correspondence form. Often, they are used to facilitate the immediate transfer to a company of some portion of a larger financing. Like letters of intent, which are generally binding in only a few particulars, letter agreements often contemplate additional documentation before additional funding is provided. For example, an investor may agree to lend a company $1 million of which $100,000 is needed immediately. This amount can be advanced when the letter agreement is signed, while the remaining $900,000 is held pending completion of the final documentation. The $100,000 will be covered by the letter agreement until the longer, final agreements are completed and signed. *See: Bridge Loans, Financing Agreements, Investment Memorandums, Letters of Intent.*

Letters of Intent are writings in correspondence form signed by a company and an investor that set out the broad parameters of the business deal between them. Letters of intent tend to be short and almost always anticipate additional formal documentation before funds are actually transferred.

Letters of intent do not appear in all financings. Some investors prefer to proceed directly from negotiations to formal financing agreements. When letters of intent are used, they always precede the formal documentation and often provide for interim working arrangements or bridge financing.

Letters of intent can be completed quickly, usually in an afternoon, and serve several purposes. First, by putting the business deal into writing, they assure both parties that the other party agrees to the major terms of the deal. Also, they usually establish a time frame for finalizing the details and getting the necessary documentation completed. Letters of intent highlight the agreements of the parties. In so doing, they tend to solidify each party's commitment to the financing and often make it easier for the parties to agree on the peripheral issues that have to be dealt with in the definitive financing agreements.

Although many people think of them as unenforceable expressions of intent, letters of intent usually contain some agreements that are binding. Some contain agreements regarding how the company will be operated until funding is provided. Other letters of intent contain binding agreements for bridge loans or other immediate funding to hold the company over until the formal financing agreements can be completed.

Most letters of intent have three things in common: They contain binding agreements by management and the company not to negotiate financing with others for thirty days or more; they allow the investor full access to company records and facilities; and they require the company to continue to operate its business in the ordinary course. Many also require management and the company to make representations about the company's business plan, financial statements, and management's stock ownership.

When preparing a letter of intent, management should be careful to understand which provisions of the letter are binding and which are not. The alteration of only a few words in a letter of intent can mean the difference between a binding obligation and a simple statement of intent.

Management also should be careful to understand the full implications of the proposed funding. Letters of intent set the tone for the negotiations of the final financing agreements. Because of this, it can be very difficult to change a poorly considered term even though that term may appear only as an expression of intent.

Managements who plan to use an attorney or other adviser in connection with the final financing agreements should consult with that adviser before letters of intent are negotiated and signed. Many entrepreneurs, however, sign letters of intent without first consulting their advisers. Some do so with the belief that they can fix what they do not like in the final documents. Others feel compelled to sign immediately when presented with an investor's letter to show their good faith and to get the deal moving. Most are disappointed later when the investor resists fixing the deal or when they discover the full impact of concessions they have made. These disappointments can usually be avoided by taking twenty-four hours to consider the letter before signing. During this time the entrepreneur can meet with his advisers to be sure he fully understands the investor's offer and has addressed the business issues that need attention. *See: Bridge Loans, Commitment Letters, Financing Agreements, Investment Memorandums, Lawyers, Letter Agreements, Negotiation, Structure.*

Sample Letter of Intent

September 2, 1993

Virden NewCo, Inc.
New Business Street
Atlanta, Georgia 33333

Attention: Harold Peters and Paul Carrot

Gentlemen:

This letter is to set forth our understanding regarding the investment by Nokomis-Atlanta Ventures Ltd., a Georgia limited partnership (the "Investor") of $1,500,000 in Virden NewCo, Inc., a Delaware corporation (the "Company"), whose sole shareholders are Harold Peters and Paul Carrot (collectively, the "Shareholders"). Except with respect to paragraphs 8, 9, and 10, the provisions of this letter are not intended to be legally binding,

1. Upon execution and delivery of the Agreement described in paragraph 7 by the Company and the Shareholders, the Investors will immediately (i) pay to the Company the sum of $850,000, and (ii) execute and deliver to the Company subscription agreements in Company's standard form subscribing for a total of 16.7 percent of the total issued and outstanding common stock of the Company after such issuance. The Company shall thereupon issue to the Investor 1,500 shares of its common stock, $.01 par value, equal in number to 16.7 percent of the issued and outstanding shares of common stock of the Company immediately after the issuance thereof.

2. In addition to the investments set forth in Paragraph 1, the Investor will invest an additional $650,000 in the Company in return for common stock which increases the Investor's percentage of the issued and outstanding capital stock of the Company immediately after such issuance by 8.3 percent (so that the Investor's total percentage ownership at that time will

be 25 percent of the issued and outstanding capital stock of the Company). This subsequent $650,000 investment will be made only after the Company has achieved certain agreed upon benchmarks, including benchmarks relating to the receipt by the Company of its first order, the first shipment of Company product and the first collection on account by the Company.

3. The Investor and each of the Shareholders will agree to vote their shares of common stock in the Company to elect a slate of directors nominated by the Shareholders, which slate of directors shall always include at least one nominee of the Investor. This agreement will be evidenced by a written voting agreement and expire upon the earlier of February 2, 1998, the sale of the Company to any third party, or the sale by the Company of shares of its common stock in a public offering. All shares of common stock of the Company issued to the Investor and the Shareholders will be marked to bear appropriate restrictive legends, including reference to the voting agreement.

4. The Company will use the $850,000 provided pursuant to paragraph 1 only to fund product development, marketing, and inventory expansion associated with the Company's software virus prevention program (the "Failsafe System"). Each of the Shareholders also agrees to submit to a physical examination at the Investor's request for the purpose of enabling the Company to acquire key man insurance. The Company further agrees to purchase key man insurance on each of the Shareholders in amounts reasonably required by the Investor.

5. The Investor will be entitled to one demand registration, at the cost and expense of Investor, and to participate as a selling shareholder in any public offerings of the common stock of the Company initiated by the Company upon reasonable terms and conditions to be agreed upon and set forth in the Agreement described in Paragraph 7 below.

6. As an inducement to the Investor to enter into this letter and the subsequent Agreement contem-

plated herein, the Company and the Shareholders, jointly and severally, represent and warrant that (i) the total issued and outstanding capital stock of the Company consists of 7,500 shares of the Company's common stock, $.01 par value, all of which are held by the Shareholders, (ii) to their knowledge, the business plan of the Company heretofore delivered to the Investor (the "Business Plan") and all other written information provided to the Investor by the Company do not contain any untrue statement of material fact or omit to state any material fact which is necessary in order to make the statements contained therein not misleading in light of the circumstances under which they are made, (iii) to their knowledge, the financial projections contained in the Business Plan have been prepared accurately based on the assumptions described therein, (iv) the Shareholders have no rights (and know of no other party having any right) in or to the Failsafe System other than by virtue of their stock ownership in the Company, and (v) that within 14 days after the date of this letter the Shareholders will each have entered into written agreements in form reasonably acceptable to Investor (A) not to use or disclose any of the confidential information or trade secrets of the Company, including information relating to the Failsafe System, except for the benefit of the Company and in the ordinary course of Company business, and (B) not to compete with the Company for a period of two years after their employment with the Company terminates for any reason.

7. The terms and conditions governing the transactions described in Paragraphs 2 through 9 hereof are to be set forth in a definitive agreement (the "Agreement"), which shall be subject to the approval of all of the parties and their counsel. Such terms and conditions shall include among others:

(a) warranties, representations and indemnities including those usually given in transactions of the nature herein contemplated, satisfactory to the Investor relating to the Company's structure, organization, business, operations and financial condition;

(b) the usual conditions which must be satisfied before parties to transactions of the type contemplated are obligated to close, including, but not limited to, obtaining of any required consents relating to material contracts, the absence of any litigation or other legal proceeding relating to this transaction or the Company; and

(c) provisions relating to compliance with all applicable securities laws.

8. All the parties agree to use their reasonable best efforts to complete the aforesaid Agreement within 30 days. Neither the Shareholders, the Company, nor the Company's management will enter into any negotiations with any third parties for the provision of the moneys described herein during the aforesaid 30-day period.

9. Following execution of the letter, the Company will provide the Investor and its agents with full and complete access to its property, books and records and will allow the Investor and its agents to talk to personnel, customers, and independent providers of professional services to the Company. The Investor agrees to hold all information obtained by virtue of such access in confidence and not to release it to third parties without the prior written consent of the Company.

10. From the date of execution of this letter, the Company will operate its business in the manner described in the Business Plan and will use its best efforts to (i) secure at least $600,000 in borrowed funds for the Company (even if such borrowing requires the personal guarantees of the Shareholders), (ii) maintain its business as a going concern, and (iii) maintain its business relationships.

If the foregoing accurately describes our understandings and agreements, please sign, date, and return the enclosed copy of this letter to me.

Sincerely,

Nokomis-Atlanta Ventures, Ltd.
(the "Investor")

By:
Floyd Williams, General Partner

Read and Agreed to this
5th day of September, 1993:

Virden Newco, Inc. (the "Company")

By:
Its:

Shareholders:
Harold Peters

Paul Carrot

Leverage refers to using debt instead of equity to increase company funds. Usually, leverage is used to avoid "giving up" equity. The cost of preserving equity is the debt service payments required to service the company's loans. These payments reduce earnings and require funding themselves. A company that has high debt in relation to its equity is said to be highly leveraged.

Leverage is used also to refer to a strong negotiating position caused by a compelling need of the other party. If a company cannot meet a large loan payment without an investor's funding, that investor may use his leverage to obtain concessions from the company he might not otherwise obtain. *See: Bridge Loans, Cash Flow, Cram Down, Debt Service, Leveraged Buyout (LBO), Negotiation.*

Licensing is an arrangement whereby an inventor grants another person or company the right to make, use, or sell his invention. In many cases, licensing is a viable alternative to starting a company and raising capital. Licensing of an invention can be very profitable to the inventor if the invention succeeds in the marketplace and the license agreement is properly structured.

In general, an inventor who licenses his technology to another stands to earn less from his invention than an inventor who builds a new company to exploit it. This is because the inventor transfers the risk and cost of developing and marketing his invention to the licensee. On the other hand, because the inventor does not undertake the time-consuming job of starting and financing a new company, his time is available to explore other interests and develop other products, which may provide additional commercial successes.

Sometimes an inventor does better to license his product instead of trying to build a new company around it. If the product requires a large capital investment or if the marketplace for it is dominated by a strong competitor, the inventor may be more successful licensing his invention than trying to raise venture capital to start a new company. If the channels of distribution are particularly hard to penetrate or name recognition is especially important to his type of product, it may make more sense to license. In short, when the entrepreneur conducts his market research, he should consider carefully whether his product is one that can be successfully developed and marketed by a new company or whether there are factors that indicate that licensing would be more fruitful. *See: Business Plan Format, Franchising, Market Research, Patents, Software Protection, Trade Secrets.*

Limited Partnerships are a form of business organization that combines attributes of corporations with those of partnerships. Like corporations, they can provide investors with the protection of limited liability. Like partnerships, they can give management and the investors flexibility in allocating profits and losses among partners.

The limited partnership is the structure most frequently used by venture capital firms to raise money. It enables investors to receive the profits and losses generated by the fund's investment without the intervention of corporate income tax. At the same time, limited partnerships give investors the flexibility needed to attract competent fund managers by funding their expenses and salaries and providing them with a percentage of profits for incentive. They are also used by young companies to transfer company losses to investors as a method of attracting equity. Transferring losses reduces an investor's after-tax cost of providing the equity.

Limited partnerships have two types of partners: general and limited. Limited partners traditionally provide funding to the entity and, by virtue of their limited partnership status, receive limited liability much like that of a corporate shareholder. The general partners do not receive limited liability and customarily manage the business. Limited partners, unlike corporate shareholders, are generally prohibited from becoming involved with the active management of the partnership. If they do become involved, they risk being treated like general partners and becoming personally liable for the actions of the entity.

Limited partnerships must be structured carefully. Obtaining the tax benefits of a limited partnership depends upon close compliance with IRS rules that govern, for tax purposes, the differences between corporations and partnerships. A limited partnership must qualify as a partnership to obtain the special tax treatment.

There are generally four factors the IRS looks at when determining how to tax a limited partnership: (1) unlimited personal liability for the debts of the entity; (2) lack of centralized management; (3) limited duration; and (4) restricted transferability of ownership interest. If a limited partnership meets fewer than two of these standards, it may be characterized and taxed as a corporation. To avoid this result, limited partnership agreements usually try to qualify under criteria (3) and (4) by making the partnership terminate after a specified period of time and restricting the rights of limited partners to transfer their partnership interests. Whenever a limited partnership is used, management should consult with its attorneys and accountants. Only they can ensure that management obtains the desired tax results. *See: R & D Partnerships, S Corporations.*

Liquidity Agreements are undertakings that help a stockholder convert his company investment into cash. They usually appear as provisions in a written contract between a company and its investor. Liquidity agreements are common in venture capital financings, particularly when the investor is uncertain whether the company will ever be able to offer its stock for sale in the public markets (i.e., "go public"). Since many venture capital investments end up being less successful than predicted by the company's business plan, these agreements can be very important to investors.

Common liquidity agreements include puts, which enable an investor to force a company to repurchase his shares for an agreed-upon price, and buy-sell agreements, which enable an investor to force management to either purchase his shares or sell its shares to him. These buy-sell arrangements make it easier for an investor to liquidate his investment even when management chooses to sell its shares. This is because it is usually easier to sell a controlling interest in a company than it is to sell a minority interest (which is what most outside investors hold).

Convertible debentures also increase investor liquidity and provide an escape when a company is not living up to expectations. They do so by giving the investor the option of not converting his debenture into shares of the company's common stock. If the company does not do well enough to give the investor a "healthy" profit upon the sale of the common stock he would obtain by converting his debenture, the investor can choose to forgo converting to the company's stock and collect instead the interest and principal repayment on his debenture.

Demand registration rights that enable an investor to force a company to register his shares for sale to the public are also a form of liquidity agreement. Debentures and promissory notes used in a financing structure provide liquidity by allowing investors to withdraw a part of their investment as a nontaxable return of debt. Any agreement that makes it easier for investors to get their money back is a liquidity agreement.

All liquidity agreements should be considered carefully before they are agreed to. Each, in creating liquidity for an investor, creates a corresponding company need for funding. If the provisions are not carefully considered, this need for funding could come at a time when it is particularly costly or unavailable. In this situation, a liquidity agreement could cripple a company or even force management out. *See: Buy-Sell Agreements, Cashing Out (or In), Convertible Securities, Co-Sale Agreements, Debentures, Demand Rights, Exits, Financing Agreements, Piggyback Rights, Puts, Registration Rights, Structure.*

LLCs (Limited Liability Companies) are a new form of business entity first created in Wyoming in 1977, which combine attributes of partnerships with attributes of corporations. They are designed to provide the ownership and tax flexibility of partnerships with the limited liability feature of corporations.

LLCs are owned by members who finance the business much like a partnership and who operate or delegate operational authority to elected managers. The principal organizational charter is the "operating agreement," which sets out the company's membership and operational rules. Membership interests typically are transferable only with the approval of other members after all requirements of the operational agreement are met. Profits and losses are shared (and taxed) to the members in the manner provided in the operating agreement.

Since the IRS officially classified the Wyoming limited liability company as a partnership for tax purposes in 1988, at least 15 other states have adopted LLC statutes and many others have amended their laws to permit LLC to do business in their states while maintaining the limited liability characteristics of corporations.

Notwithstanding this trend, LLCs are still infrequently used by growing companies because of the limited transferability of membership interests (which could make going public impossible and could dampen the enthusiasm of investors who are concerned about a clear exit plan) and because of the uncertainty over whether limited liability will be afforded their activities in states which have not adopted LLC statutes. *See: Corporations, Joint Ventures, Limited Partnerships, S Corporations, Strategic Partnerships.*

Comparison of Business Entities

	C Corporation	S Corporation	Limited Partnership	LLC
Investors	shareholders	shareholders	partners	members
Management	directors/officers	directors/officers	general partner	managers
Liability	limited	limited	limited (unlimited to general partner)	limited where recognized
Earnings Taxed To	corporation	shareholders	partners	members
Profits/Losses Allocated To	corporation	shareholders pro rata to ownership	as provided in partnership agreement	as provided in operating agreement
Limits on Transferring Ownership (other than by securities laws)	none	none	yes, in partnership agreement	yes, in operating agreement

M

Management Agreements are contracts that determine the manner in which companies will be managed. They can be in the form of shareholder agreements, which guarantee elections of management-controlled boards of directors, or in the form of contracts between companies and managements, which entitle managements to operate companies for a specified term. Management agreements often terminate if managements fail to operate companies as planned.

The term "management agreements" is misused by some investment firms to refer to consulting or management participation agreements they require a company to sign as a condition of funding. These management agreements usually require the company to pay the investor a regular fee and give him the right to obtain financial reports and participate in management decisions.

Most venture capitalists do not require these management agreements. Instead, they work their rights to participate in management into their financing agreements and do not charge a separate management fee. Whenever a management fee is required by an investor, management should consider it as a part of its cost of capital. *See: Consulting Agreements, Financing Agreements, Pricing, ROI (Return on Investment).*

Management Team refers to the group of individuals who are collectively responsible for the decision making and growth of a company. In many entrepreneurial companies the management team consists of the founders and one or two key individuals hired after the company was incorporated. Most venture capitalists prefer to invest in management teams rather than in individual entrepreneurs. This is because few individuals possess the ability or stamina that is necessary to create and manage an emerging growth company alone.

Investors usually look to the three or four people who are essential to a company's success as its management team. Most prefer to invest in companies whose management teams are complete. Because of this, the chances of obtaining venture capital are improved greatly by presenting a complete team in the business plan.

Companies with gaps in their management teams should be ready to explain what plans they have to fill the vacant spots. Most investors will want to know about these plans and how present management believes it can fill the important vacancies. Some venture capitalists help entrepreneurs fill those spots, but, as a rule, it is better to present an investor with a complete management team or with concrete plans to identify and attract additional team members.

In fact, a substantial risk many young companies face is the inability to identify and retain key personnel. Especially in high-tech fields such as bio- or medical engineering, few persons with the requisite skills may be available. Thus, presenting a business plan that lacks key players may make an investor reluctant. *See: Entrepreneurs, Five Factors.*

Market Price Method is a common valuation method used by investors who invest in growing private companies. A description of the method is contained in the *Pricing* entry. Another common method is the discounted cash flow method. *See: Discounted Cash Flow, Pricing.*

Market Research is empirical information that helps to determine whether a company's product will sell and whether the marketplace for the product is large enough to support the sales projected by the company. Every venture capitalist bases his investment decision, at least theoretically, on market research.

Market research requires an investigation of the market in which the company's product will compete and an analysis of how the company's product will fit into that market. It identifies who the company's competitors are, what their present and future products will look like and sell for, and how price sensitive its customers are. It also determines who the potential company suppliers will be and whether product components will be difficult to obtain.

Market research should include reviews of available industry data, including industry magazines and reports by industry experts. Annual reports of competitors should also be digested. And personal interviews and discussion should not be overlooked. Some of the most insightful information can be obtained by a telephone conversation with a potential competitor.

Venture capitalists conduct thorough market research and expect thorough research from the entrepreneurs they consider for their portfolios. The thoroughness of management's market research and the conclusions drawn from it should be fully reflected in the company's business plan. Unless the research is thorough and reflected in the company's business plan, few venture capitalists will invest.

If market research is new to company management, experienced consultants can be hired to help focus the questions and to conduct the research. Another way to determine what questions to research is to review one or two business plan formats and draw questions from there. *See: Business Plan, Business Plan Format, Due Diligence.*

MBO (Management Buyout) refers to a leveraged buy-out conducted by a companies existing management. *See: Leveraged Buyout (LBO).*

MESBICs (Minority Enterprise Small Business Investment Companies) are government-chartered venture firms that can invest only in companies that are at least 51 percent owned by members of a minority group or persons recognized by the rules that govern MESBICs to be "economically disadvantaged." These funds must have private capital of at least $300,000. MESBICs borrow government moneys to increase (leverage) the size of their funds just as SBICs do. As a result, most of the investment characteristics of SBICs also apply to MESBICs. *See: SBICs (Small Business Investment Companies).*

Mezzanine Financing refers to an investment provided to a company that is already producing and selling a product or service. The purpose of mezzanine financing is to help the company achieve a critical objective (such as increasing inventories to accomplish greater sales) that will enable it to go public.

Mezzanine financings are typically undertaken when they promise to decrease the company's overall cost of financing by helping the company attract a significantly better price for its shares in a later public offering. Sometimes mezzanine financings are undertaken because the market for public offerings is so poor that going public is not a viable alternative.

A theory espoused by many underwriters and investment bankers is that there are important psychological break points in initial public offerings below which the company's stock will not attract institutional investors and other important investors. Without their interest, so the theory goes, the stock will have fewer potential buyers and will obtain a lower price.

Many investment bankers believe that a company needs to offer at least 500,000 to 1,000,000 shares of its stock to support the active trading of its shares that is necessary to support a good price. A price of between $10 and $20 is considered ideal to attract the large investment banking firms and institutional investors. A price below $5, the theory goes, decreases the attractiveness of the company's shares. Since the number of company shares can be changed easily by stock splits, the critical factor in determining a viable price of a company's stock usually becomes the size of the company, its earnings history, its prospects for continued and dramatic growth, and the price-earnings ratio its shares can command.

Sometimes a mezzanine financing can move a company into a position in which its stock will attract a significantly larger audience and healthier price. By accepting mezzanine funding, management hopes to make its stock more appealing to investors and to decrease the company's overall cost of financing by making its first round of public financing significantly less costly. A large increase in the price the public is willing to pay for a company's stock means the company will have to issue fewer shares to raise funds than it would if its shares supported a lower market value. *See: Going Public, Investment Bankers, Penny Stock.*

Minority Shareholder refers to an investor who does not own enough stock to elect a majority of a company's board of directors and so cannot control the manner in which the company is run. However, in some cases, a minority shareholder may represent a "swing" vote in battles for control or may have contractual rights to participate or veto certain actions within a company. *See: Control, Shareholders' Agreements, Voting Agreements.*

N

NASBIC (National Association of Small Business Investment Companies) is an organization that maintains a directory of investment firms that are licensed by the United States Small Business Administration (SBA). Obtain a copy of the list by writing: NASBIC, 1199 N. Fairfax Street, Suite 200, Alexandria, VA 22314, or by calling (703) 683-1601. *See: National Venture Capital Association.*

National Venture Capital Association is a trade association of venture capital companies. Most members are not affiliated with the United States Small Business Administration (SBA). A list of its members can be obtained by writing the association at 1655 North Fort Myer Drive, Arlington, VA 22209, or by calling (703) 351-5267. *See: NASBIC (National Association of Small Business Investment Companies).*

Negative Covenants refer to operating covenants which prohibit a company from taking specified actions without the consent of the investor. They are a regular part of venture financings and are designed to protect the investor from future events that may dilute or undermine the value of his investment. Since they also limit management's flexibility, negative covenants should be negotiated carefully. They usually appear as part of the financing agreement.

Negative covenants typically prohibit the company from taking the following types of actions without investor consent:

- Altering the company's charter or bylaws.
- Changing the character of the business conducted by the company.
- Paying dividends, issuing new stock, or borrowing funds that are convertible into stock.
- Altering any preferences (special voting rights, rights to receive dividends, or rights to receive funds first in liquidation) contained in the stock acquired by the investor.
- Disposing of company assets or acquiring new assets in transactions that fall outside the ordinary course of the company's business.
- Voluntarily dissolving or winding up the company.
- Entering into business transactions with management of the company.

See: Affirmative Covenants, Management Agreements, Operating Covenants, Reps and Warranties, Structure.

Negotiation is the discussion, sometimes lengthy, of the terms of investor financing. It begins when management makes its first contact with an investor.

Whether that contact is face to face or made through the mail, the first impression management makes sets the tone for the dialogue with the investor. A solid presentation by management sets the groundwork for a positive exchange with the investor by improving his perception of the company and its management. This, in turn, can help reduce a company's cost for funds and improve the terms of the company's deal.

Most venture capitalists prefer to make a funding proposal to management rather than react to a proposal prepared by the company. Their proposal is made only after they complete their due diligence, during which management's opinions and expectations about financing are solicited. Usually, the proposal is specific as to amount of money, timing of investments, and the number and types of company securities the investor desires.

Once the proposal is made, management's negotiating position is reduced to that of reacting to the proposal and trying to convince the investor to modify those terms that are unacceptable. This can prove difficult, especially when a company's need for money is acute and there are no other offers on the table. Therefore, one good strategy for improving management's bargaining position and the results of its negotiation is to begin the search for money early and to approach several investors simultaneously. The entrepreneur who waits until the last minute before he approaches investors seriously compromises his ability to negotiate effectively.

Another good strategy is to convince the investor that the company presents an exceptional and rare opportunity. (This too is usually best done before the investor makes his funding proposal.) The care management takes in preparing its plans and presentations to investors pays off in better financing packages and easier negotiations. An investor's impression of the company and his judgment as to its value usually have more to do with the price he requires for his funding than all the persuasion attempted during the negotiation of the actual financing agreements. As a result, much of management's most effective negotiation usually occurs when it is selling its concept to the investor, long before formal negotiation of the terms of that financing begins.

That is not to say, however, that management should relax once a funding proposal is made and accept whatever price and structure an investor proposes. Most investors are interested in getting the best deal they can and will propose a price and structure that is favorable to themselves. Management should expect this and analyze the investor's proposal carefully, using the analysis as the basis for its negotiation with investors.

Most investors expect a reasoned, issues-oriented negotiating approach from management in which management and the investor openly address the concerns of both parties and search creatively for solutions that build a workable deal. Negotiating effectively in this context requires an understanding of venture capital deals and structures, of the needs and concerns of the company and its management, and of the perspective of the investor.

A major purpose of this book has been to provide entrepreneurs with more knowledge about the venture capital deal structuring process so that they can understand better the compromises and concessions they are asked to make. A better understanding helps management identify and articulate its concerns with objectionable parts of an investor's proposal, which, in turn, makes it easier for the parties to discuss the open deal points and arrive at acceptable compromises.

Obtaining a better understanding of a proposed deal and its short-term and long-term effects involves more than just reading one book and looking closely at the investor's proposal. It also involves getting qualified professional help from someone who has done venture deals before and can give management an independent appraisal of the proposed deal. This person should be able to guide management in suggesting effective solutions to many of the problems identified in the deal proposal. He should be conversant in the applicable securities laws so he can direct the deal's structure in a way that avoids securities problems for management and the company.

In most cases this person should be a lawyer. It simply is not true for most entrepreneurs that they can negotiate a commercially reasonable financing package without the help of a qualified professional. In most cases, the professional investor has vast deal-making experience, while the entrepreneur has little or none in structuring a funding. This, coupled with the far-reaching and often prejudicial effects of many common venture deal provisions, makes it almost foolhardy to complete a venture deal without qualified professional help.

And, while it is true that most venture investors use a reasoned analysis approach in their negotiations, entrepreneurs should not be so naive as to believe that investors will not also use deceptive tactics and pressure strategies to get the deal they want. While most effective deal makers find that an open, analytical approach makes for the best deals, some also view games and pressure tactics as a legitimate part of the negotiating process. Many of these investors mix these tactics into an otherwise straightforward negotiation. They may include delay, refusals to discuss reasons (*See: We Always Do It This Way*), and last-minute demands for concessions to "get the deal done." An adviser who is practiced at venture deal making usually can distinguish these tactics from the heart of the negotiating process so they can be dealt with effectively.

The discussion in the *Equity Penalties* entry describes one last-minute demand tactic in an otherwise open negotiation with one of the senior fund managers of a nationally prominent venture capital firm. In that case, the entrepreneur received a phone call late Friday night from the fund manager saying he could not close the deal on Tuesday unless the entrepreneur agreed to give him significantly more stock if the company did not meet its plan. The deal had been negotiated at length and was ready to be closed. The investor had numerous opportunities to raise this issue before but waited, instead, to bring it up at the last minute, to couple it with a threat not to fund, and to do so in a manner that made it difficult for the entrepreneur to get his counsel's advice.

The entrepreneur should have called his lawyer at home. Instead, he worried all weekend about his deal dying. On Monday morning, when he called his lawyers, he had convinced himself to make the concession in order "to get the deal done."

The investor's proposal was absurd, particularly in view of the manner in which it was made. It smacked of bad faith. The entrepreneur's lawyers counseled him to reject the proposal in a way that showed how ludicrous it was. The entrepreneur contacted the fund manager and told him he could not go forward with the equity penalty proposed, that it was unfair, and that if an equity penalty was critical, the parties would also have to discuss an equity bonus to management (and corresponding dilution of the investor's interest) if the company met its plan. The investor promptly dropped his demand and closed the next day.

There are several good books on negotiation. Two examples are *Getting to Yes* by Roger Fisher and William Ury and *Getting Together—Building a Relationship That Gets to Yes* by Roger Fisher and Scott Brown. Both books are a result of research conducted by the Harvard Negotiation Project and describe a constructive, issues-oriented approach to negotiation. *See: Deal Breakers, Financing Agreements, Golden Rule,*

K.I.S.S., Lawyers, Letters of Intent, Pricing, ROI (Return on Investment), Shopping, Structure.

Networking refers to a method many investors use to identify viable companies and syndicate investments. Networking refers to sharing information and prospects with other investors and persons involved in the venture capital process. Networks can be as informal as loosely knit associations among investors and their consultants or as formal as a trade association or networking organization. Many venture capital clubs provide regular opportunities for investors, and sometimes entrepreneurs, to meet and discuss mutual opportunities. Incubators and technology development centers also provide a base of networking for entrepreneurs.

Networking is important. Many investors will not consider an investment unless it is presented to them by someone they know. Certainly, most investors are more likely to consider a business plan seriously if it is recommended to them by someone they trust. Business plans that come unannounced through the mail have less chance of being read than those that are accompanied by a call from a friend or acquaintance.

Entrepreneurs should recognize the existence and importance of networking when they solicit funding. Whenever possible, entrepreneurs should use an introduction or an acquaintance to help them get the attention of an investor. Often the best way to become a part of a community's venture network is to join an incubator or attend chamber of commerce or local development authority meetings. Sometimes the right banker, accountant, or attorney (one who deals regularly with venture capital) can introduce the entrepreneur to the area's network. *See: Deal Flow,*

Incubators, Shopping, Technology Development Centers, Venture Capital Conferences.

Noncompete Agreements are contracts that discourage employees from leaving their employers by preventing them from performing similar jobs for competitors. They are used by many companies to encourage key employees to remain with the company and to prevent them from competing with it after they leave. Many venture capitalists require noncompete agreements from top management as a condition of funding. Investors often combine stock vesting agreements and stock bonus plans with noncompete agreements to ensure management loyalty. Trade secrecy and confidentiality agreements are also commonly included in noncompete agreements.

To be enforceable, noncompete agreements need to be drafted carefully. Courts dislike noncompete agreements because they interfere with a person's ability to earn a living. As a rule, courts will enforce them only when their provisions are carefully limited. The types of restrictions these agreements must contain to be enforceable vary from state to state. Some states' courts will not enforce any employee noncompete agreement. Others will, but only if they are entered into in connection with the sale or financing of a company. All states require noncompete agreements to be tightly drawn in compliance with the particular requirements of local law.

Although the rules vary from state to state and different states apply similar rules with different emphasis, a few principles of noncompete agreements do have general applicability. All states require noncompete agreements to be in writing and supported by valuable consideration. Most require them to be restricted as to territory and time. That is, an employee cannot be prevented from competing every-where forever.

Many states require that the competitive behavior that is restricted reflects only the activities the employee under-took for the company. Some states will not enforce a non-compete agreement that is signed after the employee joins the company unless the employee receives something sig-nificant from the company at the time. However, most states relax their rules when reviewing a noncompete agreement entered into between management and a com-pany buyer or financier.

It is difficult to draft an enforceable noncompete agree-ment, especially one that is not entered into in connection with a company financing. Only an attorney who is knowl-edgeable about his state's noncompete laws can insure that a noncompete agreement is drafted properly. If a noncom-pete agreement is important to a company or its investors, management should be sure to enlist the aid of an attorney to either draft the agreement or consult with management as to the agreement's scope and enforceability. *See: Confi-dentiality Agreements, Golden Handcuffs, ISOs (Incentive Stock Options), Options, Think Capital, Vesting Schedules.*

Nonrecourse Debt is an obligation that entitles the holder to collect only against assets pledged to that debt as collateral. A promissory note that permits the holder to take the collateral in payment of the note but not to collect from the maker personally in the event of a default would be nonrecourse debt. Sometimes investors refer to com-pany debt not guaranteed by management as nonrecourse debt in order to point out that the investor cannot look to the personal assets of individual management members to satisfy the loan. *See: Collateral, Personal Guarantees, Promis-sory Notes.*

O

Off Balance Sheet Financing refers to ways companies raise money that do not appear as loans or injections of capital on their financial statements. Popular methods of off balance sheet financing include joint ventures, R & D partnerships, and leases (rather than purchases of capital equipment).

Companies usually obtain funds in joint ventures and R & D partnerships by combining their know-how or product with a partner's money. The company may contribute its know-how to a joint venture funded by another party and receive royalties as the venture succeeds. The company may even retain significant control over how the venture operates. The arrangements can also permit the company to purchase the joint venture or the product and know-how at a future date. By using a joint venture instead of funding the project out of its own funds, the company can accomplish an important objective while preserving its cash for other purposes.

R & D partnerships work in much the same way. Generally, the company contributes know-how about a certain product to a limited partnership whose other partners contribute money to fund further development of the product. In this way the company gets its development funded without affecting its balance sheet. If the development succeeds in producing a marketable product, the company may either pay the partnership a royalty, or it can purchase the product for a price that nets the contributing partners a fair return on their investment.

Leases preserve company funds by enabling a company to use equipment or property without having to purchase it. In so doing, the company usually avoids having to come up with a substantial down payment and does not show the leased equipment as an asset on its balance sheet. As with other off balance sheet financing techniques, leases can benefit a company by permitting it to accomplish a company goal with a minimum of cash.

Off balance sheet financing often depends on the ability to transfer some tax benefit to an investor or requires a company to part with more control or ownership of its product or know-how than it would ideally like to. Sometimes the trade-off is in the upside potential to the company, with the company having to share more of the potential profit from a project to obtain off balance sheet financing than it would if it financed the activity in another way. But sometimes off balance sheet financing is the best or only alternative to keep a company project alive. When this is the case, the ability to keep a project going without depleting a company's other assets can mean more profits for the company and a better deal for the investor. *See: Cash Flow, Joint Ventures, Licensing, R & D Partnerships.*

Operating Covenants refer to agreements between an investor and management that outline undertakings management agrees to perform after the investor provides funding. They are typically made preconditions to the making of an investment.

Sometimes called "affirmative covenants" and "negative covenants," these agreements commonly include the obligation to provide the investor with regular financial reports, to maintain the company's corporate status, and to continue pursuing the company's main business objectives. Operating covenants can also require management to achieve specified goals or to refrain from engaging in specified activities. Failure to fulfill the obligations of an operating covenant can result in penalties to management. *See: Affirmative Covenants, Management Agreements, Negative Covenants, Reps and Warranties, Take Away Provisions.*

Opinion Letters are statements of counsel in correspondence form provided at the request of a party to a transaction. They contain counsel's opinion as to the manner in which the law applies to various aspects of the transaction being closed.

Venture capitalists usually require an opinion letter from the company's lawyer as a condition to funding. Commonly, these letters recite that the company is duly incorporated and qualified to conduct its business, that the company has the authority to enter into and perform its obligations under the financing agreements, that the financing agreements are valid, binding, and enforceable against the company, and that the company has no other agreements that conflict with them.

Most of these letters repeat representations the company and management make in the financing agreements. Nonetheless, venture capitalists usually require the opinion of independent counsel as to these and other matters to provide an independent check of the representations of the company and management.

Some company counsel will ask venture capitalists for a legal opinion to provide the company with similar protection. Some venture capitalists, however, object to giving the company their counsel's opinion. When they do object, it is usually on the grounds that the opinion is expensive and unnecessary.

Opinion letters can be expensive, particularly if they involve difficult issues or require extensive due diligence by a lawyer, but they are no more expensive for an investor than they are for a company. They may, however, be more important to the venture capitalist. For one thing, he puts up cash and receives in return only promises and an opportunity to participate in a company's success. As a result, he has good reason to be concerned about the details that ensure that the company's promises are enforceable.

By contrast, the company usually has more than the venture capitalist's promise in hand when the financing agreements are signed. It also has the venture capitalist's cash or, at least, a portion of the cash that has been promised.

This is not to say, however, that management should always forgo the opinion of investor's counsel. Depending upon the way in which the financing is structured, an opinion of investor's counsel on certain matters may be the best or only way management can protect itself from risk or liability. Management's counsel can usually be the best judge of whether an opinion of investor's counsel is needed. Certainly, if a large portion of the company's funding obligation is deferred, management should be more concerned about the enforceability of the investor's promises and more assertive in requesting an opinion of his counsel. *See: Financing Agreements, Structure, Vesting Schedules.*

Options are securities that entitle but do not obligate their holders to purchase company securities in the future for a predetermined price or a price determined by a formula. Because they do not obligate the holder to purchase shares, they cannot be used to ensure future financing for a company.

Venture capitalists often bargain for options when they fund a company. They do so because options enable them to increase the upside potential of their investment without obligating them to purchase additional shares from the company. Options are sometimes used by investors to provide antidilution protection. They do this by giving the investor the right to purchase securities in the future at today's price or another bargain price.

Options are used frequently to attract new employees or to reward existing management personnel. Options provide an attractive incentive for employees because they give them the opportunity to share in the value created by a company's growth. *See: First Refusal Rights (Company), Golden Handcuffs, ISOs (Incentive Stock Options), Warrants.*

P

Packages are business plans that are prepared and marketed for a company by a business consultant. Many entrepreneurs use packages to attract venture capital. They do so in most cases to avoid having to create a business plan and become involved in the funding process.

Business plans that are not prepared with the active involvement of management, however, stand little chance of attracting investors. Few brokers can present a company's business proposal well without this active involvement. And few investors will invest their money in a company whose management is not involved throughout the funding process.

Why must management participate in preparing the business plan? For one thing, it is rarely possible for a broker to know a client company as well as its management does. For another, regardless of how well informed and connected a broker may be, no savvy investor will invest in a company without dealing directly with management.

There is nothing wrong with seeking professional help in preparing a business plan or even in having a professional prepare parts of the plan as long as management actively participates in the planning process, understands the entire plan, and agrees with its form and focus. Entrepreneurs should understand that using a broker to help locate funding will not free them from becoming involved in the fund-raising. *See: Brokers, Business Plan, Due Diligence, Negotiation.*

Patents are limited government monopolies bestowed on inventors who create sufficiently novel products or processes and file the necessary applications. A grant of patent enables the inventor to prohibit others from making his invention in the United States for seventeen years. Other countries provide similar patent rights.

To obtain a patent, an inventor must file a patent application, which describes the best form of the invention and why it is an improvement on the existing state of the art. The application is made in confidence to the U.S. Patent Office, where it is examined for novelty. If a patent is issued, the invention is made public by the patent office, and the inventor relies upon the patent to prevent others from copying his invention. If a patent is not issued, the patent office makes no public disclosure, and the inventor is left to rely on the trade secrecy of the invention to protect it from being copied.

Only individuals can be inventors, and only inventors and their assignees are entitled to patent protection. As a result, it is important for companies to take steps to ensure that they obtain the patent rights to inventions developed by their employees and others hired to conduct research. Employee inventions often become the property of the employer by operation of law, but there are exceptions to this rule that depend on the scope of the employee's job responsibilities and the manner in which the invention is developed. To be certain of acquiring the patent rights to which they are entitled, companies should require their employees and consultants to enter into written agreements that clearly set out companies' rights to inventions. In many cases, these agreements can be included as part of an employment or secrecy contract.

Patents are not always the best way to protect technology for three reasons: (1) They require a high degree of "novelty" before they are available; (2) they require the inventor to disclose his invention to the public; and (3) their issuance does not guarantee their validity (and thus enforceability) against a challenge by a competitor. The high degree of "novelty" required means that many inventions may not qualify for patent protection even though they may qualify for trade secrets protection. Even for a sufficiently novel invention, the patent disclosure may enable others to reconstruct the invention and help them design around the scope of the claims in the patent. Also, patent disclosures allow others to examine the invention's patent for weaknesses that might enable them to challenge its validity. If they succeed, the inventor's patent protection will be lost, and he will be unable to protect his invention as a trade secret.

There are many situations in which a company might choose to forgo patent protection in favor of trade secrecy protection. For example, if the new product cannot be "reverse engineered" or reinvented (that is, a competitor cannot duplicate it once it appears in the marketplace), trade secrecy protection, which is not limited to seventeen years, might serve the company's interests better.

The formula for Coca-Cola is one example of a product that was better protected by keeping its ingredients secret than it would have been by applying for patent protection. If Coca-Cola had secured patent protection, its formula would now be available to everyone as a matter of law. By keeping it secret instead of securing a patent, Coca-Cola has managed to retain the exclusive rights to the formulation long after its patent monopoly would have expired.

Sometimes a new product does not warrant the cost or time necessary to secure patent protection. A newly invented process that is only one of many cost-effective methods for obtaining a certain result may not give the inventor a sufficient competitive advantage to warrant the expense of preparing and filing for a patent. If the patentable portion of a new product does not add significantly to its commercial value, or the application for the patent would require disclosing other proprietary methods that are valuable but not protectable by patent, reason may suggest that the patent process is better ignored. Sometimes a company simply cannot afford to apply for patent protection in every country in which it needs it and so forgoes it in the United States to avoid disclosing its invention to the world and losing its ability to claim the protection of secrecy elsewhere.

Any inventor who is concerned about protecting an invention should consult with an experienced attorney. An attorney who specializes in patent law can provide a complete explanation of the patent process and the advantages of choosing patents or trade secrecy to protect the invention. There are many pitfalls in the patent process, including strict time limits during which a patent application must be filed in order to qualify. Foreign patents must be timely filed also, or the ability to secure them can be lost. Only an experienced patent attorney can guide an inventor through the process without the inadvertent loss of protection. *See: Employment Contracts, Licensing, Trade Secrets.*

P/E is the common abbreviation for the price-earnings ratio. It refers to a multiple applied to a company's earnings (net operating profit after tax) to estimate its value. For example, a company with earnings of $500,000 and a P/E of twelve would have an estimated value of $6 million (or twelve times $500,000). Dividing that value by the number of outstanding shares gives an estimated value for each share of company stock. *See: Price-Earnings Ratio, Pricing.*

Penny Stock refers to publicly traded corporate shares that trade for $5 or less per share. Often, the term "penny stock" is used to indicate shares that actually trade for pennies. Penny stock also refers to an alternative form of venture financing, in which money is raised through a public offering of company stock at prices as low as ten shares for a dollar (or less). Usually, the penny stock offering is underwritten by a professional underwriter who, for a fee, structures the financing and uses his best efforts to sell the shares to the public.

In most cases, the underwriter charges a fee up front for undertaking the offering. The underwriter receives additional compensation if he successfully completes the offering. Often, the charges are steep. They reflect the level of risk the underwriter accepts in agreeing to put together the offering. As with all initial public offerings, the other costs associated with completing an offering are high as well. These include the cost of management's involvement in the public offering, the cost of preparing an offering circular and complying with federal and state securities laws, and the costs of engaging independent accountants and lawyers to complete the project.

Entrepreneurs who attempt penny stock offerings often do so in lieu of trying to raise money from private investors. Many do so because they are unable to attract funds from private investors. Others believe they can raise money more cheaply in the public market even after paying the high transaction costs associated with a public offering. Still others enter the penny stock market to increase the liquidity of their shareholdings by creating a public market for shares they may hold personally.

Whatever the reason, management should consider carefully the potential ramifications of a penny stock deal before rushing into it. Many professional venture investors view a penny stock offering as an indication of corporate weakness and hesitate to participate in a later round of funding. The large number of shareholders a penny stock offering can create can discourage later investments by venture investors by creating an unsophisticated and un-represented (by virtue of their inability to elect a repre-sentative to the company's board of directors) class of shareholders to whom the directors and controlling share-holders may have fiduciary responsibilities. A sophisti-cated investor willing to provide significant funding may want a voice in management but not the potential liability that such participation may expose him to with a large class of investors who each hold a very small percentage of the outstanding stock.

Some observers believe that selling penny stock has a depressing effect on the trading value of the company's stock in the long term. These observers contend that investors will always think of the company as a bargain-basement company whose stock price reflects its low value (as compared to companies with higher-priced stocks). Overcoming this market prejudice can be difficult and makes it harder for the price of the company's stock to increase significantly.

On the other hand, it may be true for a given company that a penny stock offering to the public can command a better price per share than a corresponding offering to private investors because the liquidity of publicly trade-able shares adds to their value. If the liquidity adds enough value to offset the high costs of conducting the offering, a penny stock offering may be the least expensive way to raise money.

When a venture investor cannot be found, a penny stock offering may be a company's only alternative for raising money. When this is the case, comparing the relative advantages of conducting a public offering to private funding may be irrelevant. However, in every other case, management should compare the two alternatives carefully before engaging an underwriter and initiating a penny stock offering. In their analysis, management should consider whether the liquidity created by a public offering will create enough extra value to offset the high transaction costs associated with such an offering and whether this extra value is worth the extra hassle associated with being a public company. In making the decision, management should also evaluate how likely it is that going public with a penny stock will depress the growth of market value for the stock and, thereby, make future financings more costly to the company than they might otherwise be. *See: Going Public, IPOs (Initial Public Offerings), Mezzanine Financing, Private Placements, Public Offerings, Reg D, Underwriters, Unit Offerings.*

Personal Guarantees are promises made by an entrepreneur that obligate him personally to repay debts defaulted upon by his corporation.

Entrepreneurs who incorporate their companies to avoid becoming personally liable for company debts are often disappointed when they look for financing. This is because many venture financings include a substantial amount of debt, and most lenders require entrepreneurs to guarantee their companies' loans personally. These guarantees require the entrepreneurs to pay off the loans if their companies default.

Not all guarantees are equal, however. Entrepreneurs should be aware of the concessions lenders sometimes make so that they can negotiate to reduce their personal exposure under their guarantees. For example, when two or more company officers are asked to guarantee a single loan, each officer may be liable to repay the entire amount of the loan or just a pro rata portion of it. It depends on how the guarantee is worded.

Also, the availability of company assets to secure part of a loan can often be used to limit a guarantee to a portion of the dollar value of the loan. On long-term loans, sometimes a provision can be obtained that cancels the guarantee upon the happening of some future event, such as the passage of time, the infusion of new equity into the company, or the payment of a portion of the loan.

Personal guarantees are not required in equity financings. Many venture financings, however, are made up of debt and equity. As a result, venture capitalists who fund companies with both debt and equity sometimes ask management to guarantee the debt portion of the financing. A personal guarantee in such a situation, however, may not be appropriate. If the funding is essentially a debt financing with attached stock rights given as a bonus, a guarantee may be unavoidable. When a financing is essentially an investment of equity with a portion recharacterized as debt to "sweeten the deal" for the investor, management is justified in objecting to guaranteeing the "debt" portion of what is really an equity financing. *See: Buy-Sell Agreements, Nonrecourse Debt.*

Phantom Stock Plans are employee benefit plans that give selected employees many of the benefits of stock ownership without actually giving them any company stock. Instead of giving key employees stock or stock options, the company adopts a phantom stock plan and credits each key employee with a number of "units" of phantom stock. Each phantom unit increases in value as the company's shares of common stock do and as dividends are declared on it.

When a plan participant retires or his rights in the plan otherwise vest, he receives an amount equal to the appreciation in value of the company's common stock plus the amount of any declared dividends. For example, if the company's common stock is worth $5 a share when the "units" are distributed and worth $10 a share when the employee's right to draw against the plan vests, the employee will receive $5 per "unit" plus any dividends that accrued to those "units" while he held them.

Phantom stock plans have certain advantages over actual stock plans. For one thing, they permit company employees to participate directly in the increased value of the company stock without giving them any voting rights. Also, they do not dilute the ownership percentages of the company's stockholders. Management can design phantom stock certificates that closely approximate actual stock certificates in appearance so that what the employees receive looks very much like the real thing. *See: Compensation and Bonus Plans, Golden Handcuffs, ISOs (Incentive Stock Options).*

Piggyback Rights entitle investors to register and sell their shares of company stock whenever the company conducts a public offering. They usually appear as provisions in a financing or shareholders' agreement. Piggyback rights are common in venture financings. Because they give investors a way to cash out all or a part of their investment, most venture capitalists insist on them.

Piggyback rights should be evidenced in a written agreement to be sure an underwriter will honor them. If management wants piggyback rights, these too should be reflected in a written agreement. Except for certain fees required by various state securities law administrators to be shared by all selling shareholders, companies usually bear the cost of investors exercising piggyback rights. *See: Cashing Out (or In), Demand Rights, Exits, Registration Rights.*

Pool refers to a limited partnership venture capital fund. The term comes from the limited partners pooling or commingling their investments to create the fund. Typically, these venture partnerships are managed by professional venture capitalists who receive between $2\frac{1}{2}$ to 3 percent of their funds under management as an annual management fee. They receive a share of the partnership's profits, commonly called "carried interest," as well. This carried interest portion provides an incentive for the venture managers to invest wisely. Typical venture fund investors include pension funds, insurance companies, corporations, and individuals. *See: Venture Capitalists.*

Preemptive Rights are entitlements that existing shareholders have to purchase new shares of stock issued by a company. In some states, these rights automatically exist unless the company's articles of incorporation specifically waive them. In other states, preemptive rights do not exist unless they are specifically granted in the company's articles of incorporation.

Preemptive rights complicate fund-raising. By forcing a company to offer its shares to existing shareholders before it offers them to outside investors, these rights can postpone the sale of company shares to outsiders. Because preemptive rights require company shares to be offered pro rata among existing shareholders, they can also delay funding from an existing investor by requiring the company to first offer a percentage of the shares the investor wants to purchase to the other existing shareholders. At best, this requirement will delay the funding. At worst, it will prevent it. If any of the existing shareholders exercise their preemptive rights, the new investor may decide not to provide funding because there are not enough shares left to purchase.

Often, companies with preemptive rights fail to follow the statutory procedures when issuing new shares. This makes it difficult to determine what preemptive rights each shareholder is entitled to. Since the company cannot issue shares that are subject to preemptive rights without first offering them to the existing shareholders according to their rights (at least not without incurring significant liability), not knowing what those rights are can create an imposing barrier to obtaining funding. Untangling such a mess can be costly and time consuming.

Sometimes preemptive rights are ignored or forgotten until the company is ready to go public. At that time the underwriter will insist on assurances from company counsel that the company can sell its stock to the general public. If existing company shareholders have preemptive rights, company counsel may be unable to give that opinion without first taking expensive and time-consuming steps to cure the problem. In some cases, a practical cure may not be available. *See: Antidilution Provisions, Charter, Dilution (Percentage), First Refusal Rights.*

Preferred Stock is a form of equity ownership in a corporation that contains preferences over common stock. Typically these preferences include rights to receive dividends before holders of common stock. Sometimes they include preferences in voting, rights to veto certain company actions, or rights to cause their shares to be redeemed. In a liquidation of the company, preferred stockholders are paid before common stockholders (but after all creditors).

When used in venture capital transactions, preferred stock often includes a convertibility feature. That is, it is exchangeable for common stock at the will of the investor or upon the happening of some event. When preferred stock has this feature, it is referred to as convertible preferred stock. *See: Common Stock, Convertible Preferred Stock, Convertible Securities, Debentures, Preferred Stock Umbrellas.*

Preferred Stock Umbrellas are venture financings in which the investors are issued convertible preferred stock while management and founding shareholders hold common stock. The structure is often used when management receives its shares at or about the same time as the outside investors. The existence of the umbrella establishes an argument that the stock purchased by the investors is worth more per share than that held by management. The need to create this argument arises whenever management shareholders pay less per share for their stock than do the outside investors in transactions that are contemporaneous or nearly contemporaneous. When they do, the IRS may treat the difference in share prices as "hidden income" to management and tax management on the amount of that difference times the number of shares purchased by them at the lower price. (If charged to the management shareholder, this hidden income may be deductible by the company if it withholds taxes from other payments to the shareholder.)

To try to avoid this result, management can add value to the shares the outside investors purchase by granting them preference rights over the common stock. Commonly, these preferences include the right to receive dividends before holders of common stock and the right to receive distributions on liquidation of the company before any is made to the holders of common stock. Further preferences and rights can be created to add value to the securities being purchased by the outside investors. To the extent additional value is given to the shares purchased by the outside investor, management can contend that a lower price per share is justified for their common shares. If this argument is successful, management can reduce or eliminate the risk of hidden taxable income.

Another way to reduce the likelihood of hidden income is to have management members purchase their shares long before the investors buy their shares. The longer the period of time between the two purchases, the easier it is to argue that the company's stock was worth less when purchased. Neither the preferred stock umbrella nor the passage of time between purchases, however, can guarantee that management shareholders will not be taxed on hidden income—both solutions only reduce the likelihood of being taxed and, then, only to the extent they create distinctions that reflect real differences in value.

Structuring a financing so that outsiders receive preferred stock while insiders receive common stock can make it easier for management to use common stock to attract and retain key personnel. This is because shares issued to employees must be issued at their fair market value, or the IRS may claim that the recipient must pay taxes on the difference between the fair market value of the stock and the purchase price. If only one class of stock has been issued, that fair market value will be equal to or more than the price per share paid by the outside investors (unless the company's per share value has decreased since the financing). If little time has transpired since the venture capital financing, or the company is growing or becoming more profitable, a lower valuation is unlikely. In other words, the issue price of the shares used to attract a new key employee will probably have to be as high or higher than the price paid by the venture investors.

If, by contrast, the outside investors are issued preferred stock, the company will be justified in issuing common stock to the new employee at a price that is lower than that paid by the venture investor because the common shares issued to the employee have fewer rights than the preferred shares. This, in turn, can make it easier for the new employee to purchase the shares and make the purchase more attractive. The justifiable difference in prices, of course, depends on a real difference between the value of the preferred shares and the common shares.

Preferred stock umbrellas should not be used for tax reasons without careful weighing of the cost to the company. This cost is the increased value given to the outside investors for their investment in order to improve management's argument that its shares were purchased at fair market value. The benefit to management in avoiding being taxed on hidden income or in being able to issue cheaper stock to new employees may or may not be real, depending on the findings of the IRS. (Other methods, such as earnups, puts, incentive stock options, stage financings, and unit offerings can be used to avoid potential hidden income problems. Often, these techniques can be used more effectively than a preferred stock umbrella.)

As a practical matter, however, many venture investors will insist on acquiring preferred stock as a condition of funding. A common venture investment vehicle is the convertible, redeemable preferred stock instrument.

In light of the complexities raised by issuing preferred stock, and the fact that the issuance itself generally only creates an argument that there is no taxable income hidden in the issuance of common stock to management at a lower price, management shareholders should review their situation carefully with experienced counsel. *See: Convertible Preferred Stock, Convertible Securities, ISOs (Incentive Stock Options), K.I.S.S., Preferred Stock, Pricing, Unit Offerings.*

Price-Earnings Ratio is the relationship of the market value of a company's stock to its earnings expressed as a fraction with the current share price as the numerator and the current per share after-tax earnings as the denominator. For example, if a company's stock sells for $10 a share and its per-share earnings for the year is $1, the company's price-earnings (or P/E) ratio is ten to one, or ten. Companies in industries that boast high P/Es make attractive investments for venture capitalists because they require fewer dollars of earnings to support a high company valuation and stock price. *See: Emerging Growth Companies, P/E, Pricing.*

P/Es by Industry
(3rd Quarter 1992 Ratios)

	High/Low
Computer Software and Services	24.5/21.0
Electronics (Instrumentation)	20.9/16.4
Entertainment	22.2/20.5
Hospital Management	21.1/17.2
Publishing Newspapers	27.9/26.5
Retail Stores—Department Stores	14.3/13.0
Retail Stores—Drug Stores	18.6/16.7
Restaurants	18.2/16.8

Excerpted from the Analyst's Handbook *by Standard & Poor's, a division of McGraw-Hill, Inc.*

Pricing refers to the methods investors use to determine the percentage of total equity they will require in return for providing a company with funding.

How much equity must a company sell to attract an investor? Unfortunately, there is no easy answer.

Venture capitalists weigh many factors when deciding how much equity they want in return for their investments. The amount of equity (or price) they want for their money depends on when they think the company can "go public" or attract a buyout, what they expect the total valuation of the company to be at that time, and how likely the company is to reach that goal on schedule. Also, they consider how much of its own money management has invested in the company, how much more money the company will need before it can support a public offering, how likely the company is to fail, and how much of the investment they will recoup if the company does fail.

Still other factors affect pricing as well. For instance, if a venture capitalist invests all of his money in stock, he will probably expect a higher percentage of equity than if he puts part of his money into stock and the rest into a senior security or debenture. An investor who puts his money into the company in stages instead of all at once can afford to take less equity since a portion of his money is invested only after the company has met goals that reduce the risk of later investments. The availability of collateral can also reduce a company's cost of funding by reducing the downside risk of the investor.

The stock market affects pricing too. If the initial public offering (IPO) market is supporting high price-earnings (P/E) ratios for businesses in the company's industry, investors are more likely to be enthusiastic and use a higher P/E when evaluating the company. This higher P/E means the company can raise its funding with fewer shares of stock. By contrast, if the market is doing poorly, investors will tend to think in terms of lower P/Es and require more shares to do the same funding.

Despite all these variables, venture capitalists do make concrete funding proposals to companies that are specific about price. How do they do it? Most often, the process goes something like this: After reviewing the company and its business, the venture capitalist determines what rate of return he thinks he needs to justify the investment. He knows what he normally requires in similar-stage investments, but in making this one he will determine whether the risks are greater than normal. If he usually requires a 40 percent compounded annual rate of return and this investment is riskier, he may require a higher rate. If the company's success is more certain, he may take less.

Having arrived at an appropriate rate of return, the investor next analyzes the company's projections to determine when he thinks the company will be ready for a public offering (or other profitable exit) and how the company should be performing by then. The sooner the venture capitalist thinks the company will be ready for a public offering, and the greater he believes its after-tax earnings will be, the lower his price for providing the funding.

After this, the investor investigates the P/Es of publicly traded businesses in the same industry as the company. Usually, this means that the venture capitalist compares the P/Es of several of the company's competitors in the present market. If there have been any recent initial public offerings by competitors, he will be most interested in the P/Es of those offerings. Although the investor is really interested in the approximate P/E when the company is ready to go public, the present P/Es of the company's competitors usually make the greatest impression on the investor. If the stocks of the industry leaders are selling at twenty times earnings, and smaller competitors are selling at between fifteen and ten times earnings, the venture capitalist will probably pick a number between fifteen and ten depending on what he expects the size of the company to be when it is ready to go public.

Once these decisions are made, the investor computes what percentage of the company's stock he needs to acquire in order to give him his rate of return based on his assumptions of value, timing, and P/Es. After this, he may adjust his percentage up or down depending on whether he feels he has adequately considered his downside risk or the likelihood that the company will not make its projections.

For example, an investor may determine that he needs a 38 percent annual rate of return; the company will be ready for its initial public offering in five years; and sales at that time will be $8 million with after-tax earnings of $800,000. A company of that size with those earnings, he believes, should support a P/E of fifteen. If the investor is asked to invest $600,000, and this amount will be sufficient to carry the company to a public offering without the need for additional equity financing, the investor would compute his price proposal by multiplying the company's projected earnings of $800,000 by the P/E of fifteen to project a value for the company of $12 million in five years. In order to obtain a 38 percent rate of return in the fifth year, the investor must receive five times the amount of his $600,000 investment, or $3 million. To do this, the investor must own 25 percent of the company's equity when it goes public in five years with a $12 million valuation.

This is a simplistic example of pricing, and it is only one way of arriving at a valuation. The actual process can be less analytical or more so. The investor can employ a number of different techniques that evaluate not only the prospect of success but also the probable value of his equity if the company is only moderately successful or unsuccessful. Factors such as the need for additional funding and the structure of the funding can complicate the pricing analysis. Nonetheless, this example portrays the fundamentals of venture capital pricing and provides management with a yardstick it can use to evaluate a venture capitalist's funding proposal.

How does management evaluate a funding proposal and negotiate a better price (that is, reduce the percentage of equity the company must sell)? First, ask the investor how he arrived at his price. Sometimes the investor will give a detailed explanation of his assumptions and method of pricing so that management can evaluate its fairness. Even if the investor is vague, often he will explain when he thinks the company will grow to a size large enough to support a public offering and what size and how profitable he thinks it will be then. He might also tell management what he thinks will be an appropriate P/E for the company.

Even without this information, management can still analyze a funding offer and respond with intelligent proposals for reducing the company's cost of capital. Consider the following scenario: Zappy Computer Co. develops and markets specialty computer software. It has current sales of $500,000 and is looking for $700,000 to fund expanded activities, which management asserts will position the company to conduct its public offering in three years. At that time, management forecasts sales of $5 million and after-tax earnings of $500,000. At present, the stock market is sluggish, and Zappy's publicly held competitors support P/Es of between five to twenty times earnings. Publicly held competitors with sales and earnings similar to Zappy's projected sales in three years are supporting P/Es of between ten and fifteen. Six months ago, when the market was bullish, similar companies were supporting P/Es of between twenty and thirty.

The venture capitalist says he thinks the company's projections are unrealistic and that it will probably not be able to support a public offering until its fourth year. At that time he thinks the company may have reached $5 million in sales and $500,000 in earnings. He offers to fund the $700,000 needed in return for 56 percent of the company's outstanding common stock.

Is the offer fair? What assumptions is the investor making? To answer these questions, management needs to conduct its own analysis of pricing.

The first thing for Zappy's management to do is pick a P/E for the purpose of estimating company value. The P/Es for similar companies range from a high of thirty in the best markets to a low of ten in sluggish ones. Assuming a P/E of ten in the worst case, the investor is asking for 56 percent of ten times the $500,000 earnings he projects the company will make in its fourth year. In other words, the venture capitalist expects a return equal to 56 percent of $5 million in four years. Assuming the lowest P/E, this means that in four years the investor expects to hold $2.8 million worth of company stock in return for making a $700,000 investment today. Stated another way, he expects to receive a return of $4 for each $1 he invested four years earlier. In percentages, this is a compounded annual rate of return of 41 percent.

Assuming a P/E of twenty makes the investor's return much higher. At this rate, the company's $500,000 earnings will be worth twenty times $500,000, or $10 million, and the venture capitalist's 56 percent will be worth $5.6 million, or eight times his original investment four years later.

Now management should evaluate the company based on its own projections and a fair but conservative

P/E. These projections assume the company will generate $500,000 of profits in its third year. If management splits the difference between the best and worst possible P/Es and uses twenty, then Zappy could be worth $10 million in three years. To give the investor a 44 percent compounded annual return on his investment would triple his money in three years. In other words, the investor's stock should then be worth three times $700,000, or $2.1 million. The percentage of stock necessary to generate this value would be 21 percent. This is much less than the 56 percent originally proposed.

Despite all the computations of management and investors, the price the venture capitalist will receive for his investment will be the one the parties agree on. The foregoing illustration, however, does give management some clues as to how it can negotiate to reduce the percentage of equity the venture capitalist will be willing to take and still do the deal. To reduce the price, management must convince the investor that some of his assumptions are unrealistically conservative or that his return on investment is too high. (The latter may be close to impossible to accomplish.)

This can best be done by discussing those assumptions with the investor. Several pricing assumptions are always open to further analysis and refinement. These include the following:

- *The P/E employed by the investor.* A higher P/E ratio would reduce the cost of the company's funding. How did the investor arrive at the P/E he chose? Have higher P/Es dominated the industry? Is his P/E based on current P/Es in a sluggish market? Does the investor really believe the low P/E he chose will prevail when the company is ready to sell its stock to the public?

- *The return on investment the venture capitalist expects to make.* Does the return his pricing proposal generates reflect the rate of return he usually requires, or is it significantly higher? Is the return on investment in line with those commonly quoted within the venture capital industry? If not, why not?

- *The future valuation of the company assumed by the investor.* How does it compare with the company's projections? Certainly, it will be less optimistic. But should not the valuation be a higher number that is closer to that projected by the company?

- *When the investor expects to be able to cash out.* Most likely this will be later than when the company projects. After all, things never go according to plan. But if the company's projections were well done, they should have provided for some of the unexpected contingencies. If they have, perhaps the investor should move his projected exit date forward.

- *What the investor thinks his downside risk is.* This may be difficult to quantify, but it plays an important role in the investor's pricing. Is his analysis of the downside realistic? Does he think company failure is more likely than it is? (Certainly, he will think it is more likely than management does.) What does he think his likely loss will be if the company fails? Should his expectations be mitigated by factors he did not adequately consider?

The price of a deal can also be reduced by changing its terms to reduce the investor's risk. For instance, if collateral can be given, the venture capitalist's downside risk will be reduced. Issuing senior securities to the investor can give him priorities in the case of liquidation and thereby reduce his risk. Recasting some of the investment as debt that will be repaid even if the company is not successful enough to support a public offering at a high P/E also reduces risk. Raising more of the needed money from other sources does the same, especially if the source is management. *See: Convertible Securities, Debentures, Discounted Cash Flow, Negotiation, P/E, Preferred Stock Umbrellas, Price-Earnings Ratio, ROI (Return on Investment).*

Private Placements are sales of company securities that do not involve a public offering and that are not required to be registered with the federal and state securities commissions. "Private placement" refers to offerings that comply with the requirements of an exemption to the registration requirements of the securities laws. In most cases, the exemption calls for the preparation of an offering memorandum that describes the company and the risks associated with investing in it. Sometimes the exemption permits a sale of a limited number of securities to certain qualified investors without a formal offering memo.

Failure to register the sale of securities or to comply with the requirements for an exemption from registration can impose serious liabilities on a company and its management. Experienced counsel should be consulted before any offering of company securities is made, including an offer to a professional venture capitalist.

Whether an offering is a private placement depends upon a number of factors, including requirements and limitations relating to the

- Number of offerees (not purchasers).
- Experience and knowledge of the offerees in making investments.
- Ability of the offerees to bear the economic risk of the investment.

- Number of securities offered.
- Size (in dollars) of the offering.
- Manner in which the offering is conducted.

The company issuing securities also bears the burden of establishing that each offeree in a private placement has had appropriate access to sufficient information about the company and is capable of fending for himself in analyzing such information to reach an investment decision. To fulfill this burden the issuing company must document the identity of each offeree, the characteristics that make him an appropriate purchaser, and the nature of his access to company information.

This requirement can be hard to meet with any certainty. This is because it requires the issuing company to make judgments about the nature of the offerees. While this may be relatively easy to do with institutional investors (such as established venture capital funds), which are clearly sophisticated and able to fend for themselves (based on the fact that they have made many other investments), judging the qualifications of individual investors is more difficult. As a general rule, individuals who are officers of the issuer or who have made similar investments before and are familiar with the issuer's operations will be easier to qualify than individuals who are not involved in the company's ongoing operations or who have not made investments in similar ventures.

Companies must also be sure that the purchasers of their securities are acquiring shares for investment and not for the purpose of redistributing them. If those purchasers, in turn, transfer the securities to others, the company may be deemed to have engaged in a public offering from the outset and to have violated the registration requirements.

In order to prevent such transfers, companies should require each purchaser in a private placement to state in writing that he is purchasing the securities for his own account and without a view to their subsequent distribution. In addition, the company should place a restrictive legend on the certificate of the securities that is delivered to the purchaser stating that the securities represented by the certificate may not be transferred unless pursuant to an effective registration statement or an exemption from the registration requirements, which is satisfactory to the company's counsel. The company should also instruct its transfer agent not to transfer any of the securities (containing the legend or not) without counsel's written approval.

It is not difficult to see that the general exemption for private placements (Section 4(2) of the 33 Act and corresponding state laws) contains subjective requirements that can be difficult for a company to fulfill with any certainty. Because of this, the Securities and Exchange Commission (SEC) and the state securities commissions have identified a number of more clearly delineated "safe harbor" exemptions that companies can use to avoid the registration requirements of the securities laws. These safe harbors set out very specific objective requirements which must be followed in order for them to apply. Because of this specificity, companies find them easier and safer to use than the general 4(2) exemption.

The federal safe harbor exemptions include the Rule 504, 505, and 506 exemptions of Regulation D (discussed in detail in the *Reg D* entry), the federal intrastate exemption, and the Regulation A exemption. In general, these exemptions provide for three types of offerings with different requirements for disclosure, investor sophistication, and maximum number of investors. One exemption permits offerings of up to $500,000, another allows offerings of up to $7.5 million, while the third contains no dollar limitation but imposes sophistication requirements on "unaccredited" investors.

The federal intrastate safe harbor provides a registration exemption for local offerings by local companies that are conducted entirely in one state. It provides objective standards companies can follow to be sure of obtaining the more general intrastate exemption contained in Section 3(a) (11) of the 33 Act. The standards are contained in Rule 147. In general, they permit sales only in the state of residence of the issuing company and only to residents of that state. They require that the issuing company derive at least 80 percent of its revenues from the state and limit resales of securities purchased in the offering. Under the rule, resales may be made only to residents of the state for a period of nine months after the offering. If any resales are made outside the state during the period, the exemption for the entire offering can be disqualified. Because of this resale requirement and the restriction of the exemption to local companies, other exemptions are more commonly used than the intrastate exemption.

The SEC's Regulation A permits offerings of up to $5 million of securities under specified conditions. To meet this exemption's requirements, a company must prepare an offering circular (unless the offering is for less than $100,000) that includes two years of financial statements. The offering circular is reviewed by the SEC much like a public offering circular. Also, as in registered public offerings, there is no limitation on the number of persons the shares may be offered or sold to and no special investor qualification requirements. Nonetheless, the Reg A exemption has historically been used infrequently because of the restrictions on the amount of money that can be raised ($1.5 million until 1992) and the expense generated by preparing the offering circular and completing the SEC review. A new question-and-answer format offering circular form was introduced by the SEC in 1992 to facilitate Reg A Offerings. *See: Blue Sky Laws, Investors, Public Offerings, Reg D, Restricted Securities, SEC (Securities and Exchange Commission), Safe Harbors, 10b5, 33 Act.*

Procrastination can sometimes help management retain more of its company's equity. As a general rule, the longer a company avoids selling stock to outsiders the less stock it will have to sell in order to raise needed funding, and the less management's stockholdings will be diluted. Put another way, the more management can accomplish without using outside equity, the better bargaining position it will be in when it eventually does look for venture capital.

There are two reasons for this. First, delaying the company's need for additional investment shows prospective investors that management can make things happen and manage cash flow wisely. Second, and more important, the more the company can achieve without outside help, the less risk an investor must take when he invests in the company.

Procrastination can also be deadly to a company's funding efforts. Raising venture capital takes time. Three to six months is not unusual. Once company management decides to raise outside capital, it should begin its efforts in earnest. *See: Cash Flow, Dilution (Percentage), Stage Financing.*

Projections are management's best estimates of how its company will progress. The word "projections" is usually used to refer to the financial estimates contained in a business plan. They are where all the narrative analyses and market research of the business plan are translated into language investors understand best: dollars and cents. In a way, they are the heart of the business plan.

Usually, projections are given in substantial detail, in the format of financial statements, and include pro forma cash flow and income statements broken out on a quarterly or monthly basis. Projections usually appear immediately after the company's historical financial data in the business plan. Most venture capitalists like to see projections carried forward three to five years.

Investors scrutinize projections. If the numbers interest them, they will question management thoroughly about the assumptions underlying the projections. The more rigorous, considered, and realistic the projections, the more likely they are to be achieved, and the more likely they are to withstand an investor's scrutiny.

Projections provide investors with a basis for determining how much equity they will require in return for funding a company. Unrealistic projections that fail to provide for foreseeable contingencies are not likely to attract funding. If a venture capitalist does offer to fund a company with unrealistic projections, it will usually be at a substantially higher price than management anticipated. By contrast, realistic projections not only help attract funding but also help management to forecast how much equity the company will have to sell to obtain funding.

Some entrepreneurs believe that having a large accounting firm review their projections will help them raise money. The theory is that such projections are more believable and, therefore, more likely to convince prospective investors to invest in the company. The fact is, however, that accountants cannot guarantee the accuracy of the assumptions underlying the projections, and investors know this. As a result, an accountant's signature near a company's projections may make an investor more comfortable with the accuracy of the arithmetic in the projections but will not make him more likely to invest. *See: Benchmarks, Business Plan Format, Pricing.*

Promissory Notes are written promises to repay money borrowed plus interest. They typically describe the amount borrowed, the interest charged, and the method for repaying the lender.

Promissory notes can be secured or unsecured. If they are secured, property (collateral) is pledged to back up the company's promise to pay. If the note is not paid on time, the lender can foreclose on the collateral and apply the proceeds to pay down the note. Unless they specify otherwise, promissory notes are assumed to be with recourse. That is, the holder of the note can collect it against the maker directly if it is not paid. If the note specifies, however, its holder can be limited to proceeding only against the collateral that secures the note.

Promissory notes can be, and often are, backed up by personal guarantees of key management members. Guarantees are commonly required by banks and lending institutions that lend to entrepreneurial companies. Promissory notes that are not secured or guaranteed are backed only by the company's promise to pay. Young companies sometimes issue unsecured notes when they borrow from friends, family, or management.

Professional venture investors often require more sophisticated debt instruments, such as debentures or debt-like instruments such as redeemable preferred stock. When they use notes, they often require management to execute guarantees. *See: Angels, Collateral, Debentures, Factoring, Inventory Financing, Nonrecourse Debt, Receivables Financing.*

Public Offering refers to a sale of company securities that is registered with the federal Securities and Exchange Commission (SEC) and state blue sky commissions. It is an offering and subsequent sale of company securities that does not rely on an exemption from the 33 Act's registration requirements. Shares issued in a public offering are freely tradeable (unless they are otherwise restricted because the holder is an insider).

Public offerings generate needed cash but are expensive and time-consuming to conduct. They also subject the company to ongoing reporting and disclosure requirements with the SEC. At the same time, however, they create a market of freely tradeable company securities that the company can use to raise capital in the future and that management or employee shareholders can use to convert their holdings into cash. Having publicly traded stock makes company shares in employee incentive plans more attractive because the shares are easier to convert into cash.

An active market for company shares makes it easier for a company to expand its activities through the acquisition of other businesses. Because they are readily convertible into cash, registered company shares can often be used instead of cash to acquire a company. With the proper deal structure, registered company shares can also be used to ease the immediate tax burden of a seller caused by his company's sale and make the acquisition easier to close. *See: Going Public, IPOs (Initial Public Offerings).*

Puts are an investor's right to force a company or another shareholder to purchase his shares for an agreed-upon price. Puts usually appear in a written agreement such as a financing or shareholders' agreement. Puts provide investors with wanted liquidity but at a significant cost to the company. Because they are exercisable at the will of the shareholder (although sometimes only after a certain event has occurred), they can be exercised at a time that is inconvenient for the company, forcing it to devote its resources to paying off the investor when it needs to devote them to its operations. For example, an investor may exercise a put of 100,000 shares of common stock when the formula put price entitles him to receive $500,000 for those shares. Without the put, management might have used that $500,000 to purchase needed equipment or to expand inventory to meet the demands of growing sales. The exercise of the put forces the company to delay its plans and to search for funds to replace the $500,000 withdrawn from the company. *See: Calls, Cash Flow, Convertible Preferred Stock, Liquidity Agreements.*

R

R & D Partnerships refer to research and development limited partnerships, which are used to obtain financing for a specific company project. In this type of arrangement, the company usually sells its rights to its product to a "limited partnership" of which it is the general or "managing" partner. The funding is used to complete development of the product. The investors expense the portion of the funding used to complete product development and use that expense to reduce their taxable income. The company retains a right to license or repurchase the product or the technology when the development work is successful.

Unfortunately, the usefulness of R & D partnerships as a device to transfer tax benefits was limited by Congress when it adopted new "passive loss" rules in the 1986 Tax Reform Act. These rules restrict the types of income against which investors can apply their losses and restrict the usefulness of any credits generated to investors. Generally speaking, investors can only use R & D partnership losses to offset income from other passive investments.

Obtaining tax benefits from an R & D partnership requires careful attention to a variety of complex and inter-related tax laws. Failure to structure the partnership correctly will lose the advantages of the R & D partnership. A qualified tax professional should be consulted before structuring any R & D partnership investment. *See: K.I.S.S., Lawyers, Limited Partnerships, Off Balance Sheet Financing, S Corporations, Structure.*

Ratchets are powerful forms of antidilution provisions which investors sometimes request in connection with fundings. In a ratchet, the investor is given additional shares of stock for free if the company later sells shares at a lower price. The number of free shares the investor receives is enough to make the investor's average cost per share (counting all of his purchased and free shares) equal to the lower price per share given to the later investor. What makes the ratchet so powerful is that the first investor is given these extra shares regardless of the number of shares purchased by the later investor.

For example, if an investor who has a ratchet purchases 100,000 shares of company stock for $200,000, or $2 a share, and the company later sells another investor 100,000 shares for $1 each, the first investor would receive another 100,000 shares for free. The result would be the same if the second investor bought only one share for $1.

Ratchets can also be tied to options or warrants. When they are, the investor receives extra shares when he exercises his option. When ratchets are tied to conversion prices, as in convertible preferred stock, the extra shares are received at conversion. Other types of antidilution provisions employ weighted average or other fairness mechanisms that give the investor fewer shares when the second investor purchases fewer shares. *See: Antidilution Provisions, Dilution (Percentage), Weighted Average Antidilution.*

Receivables Financing refers to any borrowing that is secured by a company's accounts receivable. *See: Factoring, Inventory Financing.*

Reg D refers to Regulation D of the federal Securities and Exchange Commission (SEC), which sets out certain "safe

harbor" exemptions to the 33 Act's registration requirements. These safe harbors have clearly delineated requirements that enable companies to safely sell their shares in
private or limited placements without conducting public
offerings. Because of their specificity, Reg D exemptions
are easier to rely on than the general private placement
exemption contained in Section 4(2) of the 33 Act. Whenever possible, one or more of the exemptions spelled out in
Reg D should be followed.

The provisions of Reg D are set forth in six rules, the
last three of which contain the exemptions. Because of their
importance, each of the rules is summarized below.

Rule 501. Rule 501 provides the method of calculating
the number of purchasers who can be involved in sales
conducted under the exemptions in Rules 505 and 506 and
defines the term "accredited investor" as it is used in Reg
D. Under circumstances spelled out in Reg D, sales to these
accredited investors can be made without counting them
toward the maximum number of allowable investors under the exemption. The accredited investor category consists of persons who fall within, or who the issuing
company reasonably believes fall within, one of the cate-
gories summarized below.

- A qualified bank, savings and loan association, or
  insurance company
- Certain investment companies and employee benefit plans
- A private business development company that is
  subject to the Investment Advisers Act of 1940
- A 501(c)(3) charitable organization with at least $5
  million in assets
- A director, executive officer, or general partner of
  the issuing company

- A trust with at least $5 million in assets, which is directed by a "sophisticated" person (as defined in Rule 506)
- A natural person whose net worth (individual or jointly with his spouse) exceeds $1 million
- A person who has had individual income of over $200,000 or joint income with his spouse of over $300,000 during each of the last two years
- An entity in which all of the equity owners are accredited investors

Rule 502. Rule 502 describes general conditions that must be met to secure a Reg D exemption. The rule deals with integration, information disclosure, the manner of conducting offerings, and resale limitations.

Integration

Under Rule 502(a) the SEC will not integrate (or combine) sales made more than six months prior to or after a Reg D offering so long as within such period the issuing company makes no offers or sales of a same or similar class of securities (other than under certain employee benefit plans).

Information Required

Rule 502(b) provides that no prescribed information need be furnished for offers and sales of up to $1 million under its Rule 504 exemption or where such sales are made only to accredited investors under the Rule 505 and 506 exemptions. For offers above $1 million that include nonaccredited investors, the type and degree of disclosure is linked to the size and nature of the offering under Rules 505 and 506. If the offering involves both accredited and nonaccredited investors, the issuing company must distribute the information to all investors.

Offerings of up to $2 million require disclosure of the type required by Part II of the SEC's Form 1-A. Larger offerings require more disclosure. Those to $7.5 million require distribution of the kind of information called for in Part I of Registration Form SB-2. If Form SB-2 is unavailable (e.g., if the issuer is a reporting company), the company must supply the kind of information "required in Part I of a registration statement filed under the 33 Act on the form the issuer would be entitled to use." (For most companies this will be Registration Form S-1.) Companies offering more than $7.5 million worth of securities must supply information of the type required in Part I of a registration statement.

Manner of Offering Limitations

Rule 502(c) provides that, with the exception of state-registered offerings under Rule 504, the issuing company or anyone acting on its behalf may not publicly solicit or generally advertise in connection with any offer.

Resale Limitations

Rule 502(d) requires issuers to exercise reasonable care in determining that purchasers of their securities are not engaging in illegal private resales. The reasonable care required by the rule includes (but is not limited to)

- Making a reasonable inquiry into whether the purchaser is acquiring the securities for himself or another.
- Providing written disclosure to each purchaser prior to sale that the securities are not registered under the 33 Act and cannot be resold unless registered or exempted.

- Placing a legend on the stock certificate stating that it has not been registered under the 33 Act and setting forth the restrictions imposed on the transferability of the underlying security.

Rule 503. This rule requires a written notice of sale to be filed on Form D. The issuing company must file five copies of the form within fifteen days after the first sale in order to receive a Reg D exemption. (Some states require filing before the first sale.)

Rule 504. Rule 504 provides an exemption for issuing companies that are not reporting companies or investment companies. The exemption applies to sales of up to $1 million in securities made during a twelve-month period. It prohibits the issuer from making any general advertisement or solicitation in connection with the offering and requires the filing of a timely notice on Form D. The ceiling of $1 million is reduced by the aggregate of all sales in the twelve months preceding and during the 504 offering that are made in reliance on any exemption under Section 3(b) of the 33 Act or are in violation of the registration requirements of Section 5(a).

Rule 505. Rule 505 allows an exemption for offers and sales of securities up to $5 million, subject to offsets for certain types of sales occurring within the past twelve months and throughout the Rule 505 offering. The issuing company, which cannot be an investment company, must meet the disclosure requirements set forth in Rule 502, as well as the offer and resale provisions in Rules 502(c) and (d). Although there may be an unlimited number of accredited investors, Rule 505 requires that the issuer reasonably believes that it has sold securities to no more than thirty-five nonaccredited purchasers.

Rule 506. This rule provides an exemption for limited offers and sales of securities without regard to the dollar amount of the offering. Like Rule 505, it limits the number of nonaccredited purchasers to thirty-five. Unlike Rule 505, however, Rule 506 requires that nonaccredited investors be "sophisticated" before they can purchase company securities. The language of the sophistication requirement reads as follows:

> Each purchaser who is not an accredited investor either alone or with his purchaser representative(s) has such knowledge and experience in financial and business matters that he is capable of evaluating the merits and risks of the prospective investment, or the issuer reasonably believes immediately prior to making any sale that such purchaser comes within this description.

Summary of Reg D. The safe harbor exemptions contained in Reg D are nonexclusive. That is, companies that rely on them need not rely on them exclusively. They may also rely on other exemptions, such as the general 4(2) private placement exemption, to avoid the 33 Act's registration requirements. Nonetheless, because their detailed requirements make them the safest way for companies to obtain a registration exemption, they should be used whenever possible, even in financings to a single venture capitalist.

The Reg D exemptions do not relieve a company or its management from the need to comply with the provisions of the securities laws in the states in which they offer or sell securities. Also, they do not exempt a company from the federal and state antifraud provisions, such as the 33 Act's Rule 10b5. The antifraud provisions make it necessary for issuing companies to disclose or make available to offerees material information about the issuing company and the offering even in offerings conducted under exemptions that do not require the disclosure of any prescribed information. Failure to comply with state blue sky laws or the antifraud provisions of the federal and state securities laws can impose serious liabilities on a company and its management. It can even impair a company's ability to raise money in the future.

Because of the complexity of the federal and state securities laws and the severity of the penalties for failure to comply with those laws, a company should consult experienced counsel before offering or selling any of its securities. Only a qualified professional can assure management that the company's security offering has been conducted in a manner that will not create significant liabilities for the company and its management. *See: Blue Sky Laws, Going Public, Integration, Investment Reps, Investors, IPOs (Initial Public Offerings), Private Placements, Restricted Securities, 10b5, 33 Act.*

Registration Rights entitle investors to force a company to register the investors' shares of company stock with the Securities and Exchange Commission (SEC) and state securities commissions. This registration, in turn, enables the investors to sell their shares to the public. Registration rights give investors liquidity by enabling them to free their shares from the transfer restrictions imposed on unregistered securities by the federal and state securities laws. Venture capitalists invariably require them as a condition of funding.

Registration rights come in two varieties: demand rights, which enable investors to require a company to register their shares for sale in a public offering any time an investor demands; and piggyback rights, which allow investors to include (or "piggyback") their shares in a public offering the company is already conducting.

Entrepreneurs often treat registration rights as a necessary evil and pay only cursory attention to the details of these agreements. This attitude can prove costly later on.

Management should negotiate the registration rights agreement as it would any other important part of its financing arrangements. Some important issues management should address are

- The number of demand registrations the investor can require (generally, one is enough).
- When the investor can make demand (some will refrain from making a demand for a period of time).
- Who pays for the demand registration (registrations are expensive).
- The minimum and maximum dollar size of a demand registration (the larger the minimum and smaller the maximum the better).
- Whether management shareholders can participate with the investor in demand and piggyback registrations (if they can, put it in writing).
- How often the investor can participate in a piggyback registration and how many shares he can sell.

Most companies have no trouble giving an investor piggyback registration rights as long as his rights are subject to the veto of the company's underwriter. Giving such rights does little to disrupt a company's plans and does not require the special effort of demand registrations.

Demand registrations, however, do nothing for a company after the initial funding but do require it to undertake the expensive and time-consuming effort of conducting a public offering whenever the investor demands. These offerings require significant efforts from management, diverting them from the business of running the company. They can even depress the market price of the company's stock if the offering is poorly timed. For these reasons, it pays to limit the demand registration rights as much as possible. *See: Demand Rights, Liquidity Agreements, Piggy-back Rights.*

Reports and Records refer to the monthly balance sheets, income statements, and cash flow statements that most venture capitalists require of the companies in which they invest. Investors expect these reports to be provided promptly and regularly after a funding is completed.

Well-kept records tell them what the company has done and how it is proceeding toward accomplishing its goals. The types of records a company generates (beyond balance sheets and income statements) tell investors a lot about how much control management exercises over the company and how well informed management is about its company's performance. In short, a well-maintained set of books with appropriate reporting mechanisms to management is essential to attract investors. Without these fundamental reports investors cannot evaluate the history of a company or the prospects for its success. *See: Audits, CPAs (Certified Public Accountants).*

Reps and Warranties refer to the statements of facts, opinions, and estimates investors ask companies and managements to put into writing as a condition of funding. These representations (reps) and warranties usually appear in the financing agreement. Some of the more common ones are

- *Organization and corporate power.* The company is duly organized, in good standing, and is qualified to conduct business in the manner and at the locations it is conducting business.

- *Authorization.* The company has the power and authority to enter into the financing agreements and to perform its obligations under them. The agreements have been duly authorized by the company's board of directors and by all other necessary corporate action.

- *Capitalization.* The company's outstanding shares of capital stock consist of only those disclosed in the representation. No person has any rights to acquire any capital stock in the company except those that management has described. If the company owns shares in any other companies, that ownership is disclosed as well.

- *Financial statements.* The financial statements delivered by the company to the investor are accurate, complete, and prepared in accordance with "generally accepted accounting principles."

- *Undisclosed liabilities.* The company is not subject to any material claims or liabilities that are not disclosed on its most recent balance sheet.

- *Absence of changes.* There have been no material adverse changes in the company or in its operations since the date of the last balance sheet delivered to the investor.

- *An accurate business plan.* To the best of management's knowledge, neither the company's business plan nor any other information delivered to the investor contains any untrue or misleading statements. The business plan projections were prepared based upon the assumptions disclosed therein, assumptions management believes to be reasonable.

- *Properties.* The company has good and marketable title to all of its properties.

- *Compliance with laws.* The company has complied with all laws and regulations that apply to it.
- *Taxes.* The company has filed all of its tax returns on time and has paid its taxes.
- *Contracts and laws.* All of the company's material contracts have been disclosed to the investor. The company is not in default under any of its agreements. The financing agreements do not conflict with or cause a default under any of the company's other agreements, its charter, or any laws.
- *Intellectual property.* The company has sufficient title to its patents, trademarks, and copyrights to conduct its business. To management's knowledge, the company's business does not infringe upon any patents or intellectual property rights of others.
- *Litigation.* Except as has been disclosed to the investor, there is no litigation or other claim pending or threatened against the company.

Other reps regarding cost estimates, market research conclusions, and revenue projections may also be requested.

Reps and warranties should be made carefully. If they are inaccurate, they should be corrected. If they are overbroad, they should be narrowed. Otherwise, they may create a default that releases the investor from his obligations and subjects management and the company to liability. *See: Boilerplate, Investment Reps, Operating Covenants, Opinion Letters.*

Restricted Securities refer to shares of company stock that were not registered in a public offering and consequently cannot be resold or transferred until certain events occur that exempt the resale from registration or fulfill the registration requirements. Usually, the certificates for re-stricted securities bear legends identifying the limitations on their transferability. When issuing restricted securities, prudent management requires its investors to represent in writing that they are purchasing the shares for investment purposes only and do not intend to resell them.

The shares of stock a venture capitalist buys from a company are usually restricted securities. The reason for this is that most companies rely upon exemptions from the 33 Act registration requirements when selling their shares and thus do not register them. As a result, the venture investor cannot resell them without first causing the com-pany to either register the shares with the Securities and Exchange Commission (SEC) and state securities commis-sions or complying with an exemption to those registration requirements. It is for this reason that venture investors look to other devices, or exits, to enable them to liquidate, or cash out.

The shares held by management and other company shareholders are usually restricted too. Unless these share-holders negotiate rights to participate with the company's venture investor in some of its exits, they must register their shares or rely upon an exemption from registration before they can sell them. In the absence of a public offering in which they can register their shares, this usually means selling them under the provisions of SEC's Rule 144. This rule identifies circumstances in which restricted securities may be sold. In general, it allows holders of restricted securities who have held their securities for two years after they have paid for them to sell in any three-month period a number of their shares no greater than the larger of

> 1 percent of the total number of shares of their class of stock then outstanding or, if the security is listed on a national exchange or quoted on the National Associa-tion of Securities Dealers Automated Quotations

(NASDAQ), the average weekly trading volume of their class of stock.

After three years, most resale restrictions lapse for persons who are not significant shareholders or members of company management. State securities laws and other rules relating to insider trading and certain SEC reporting requirements must, however, be complied with before any restricted security is sold. Because of the complexity of these laws, any holder of restricted securities should consult an attorney before transferring ownership of his stock. *See: Exits, Going Public, Investment Reps, IPOs (Initial Public Offerings), Legend Stock Liquidity Agreements, Private Placements, Reg D, Registration Rights.*

Revenue Participations refer to financing structures that give an investor the right to receive a percentage of company sales or revenues. Revenue participations work like royalties: The company pays the investor an agreed-upon percentage of sales and deducts the payments as a business expense. The investor shows the payment as ordinary income. Unlike royalties, however, revenue participations usually grant a percentage of all sales instead of just those on a particular product. Revenue participations can be reflected in a written agreement or in a certificate, sometimes referred to as an RPC.

Sharing a percentage of revenue with an investor can accomplish some interesting results. First, the investor may become less concerned with the company maximizing earnings (profits) because he is paid based on sales. Second, management's attention may be focused on maximizing profits by minimizing expenses, so that its projected profit margin can be realized after the participation payment is made. Third, the investor may be less concerned with controlling or participating in company affairs. He may not even require a seat on the board or audited financial statements, at least as long as he is being paid and things are running smoothly. He will, of course, expect regular payments and regular statements of sales. Fourth, the entrepreneur gives up no equity.

The terms of a revenue participation should be negotiated carefully so that it will not create a cash flow crisis. Payments should not "kick in," or be triggered, until agreed-upon levels of sales revenue are accomplished in order to ensure that the company can handle the drain on cash flow caused by the revenue participations. RPCs can also be made convertible or be ratcheted, so that the investor's percentage increases or decreases according to predetermined sales levels. In all events, revenue participations should be capped so that the company's obligations expire once the investor has obtained the return he bargained for.

Revenue participations are not too common, but they do have their advocates among investors. According to Arthur Lipper III, a venture capitalist and former chairman of *Venture* Magazine,

> One of the reasons I like to use the revenue participation certificate method of investing in private companies is that matters of management perks are then of no concern to me. The entrepreneur should be free to live well "on the company" and spend as he feels justified without fear of shareholder or profit-interest holder criticism. That's fine as long as every week, month, or quarter I receive the agreed-upon share of revenues. I fly economy class, and I expect others spending my money to do so also if my interest (and reason for my assuming financial risk) in their activities is profit-related.

Revenue participations may become more common in the future. One reason many venture capital funds have historically invested in equity was to take advantage of lower capital gains rates on the profits they obtain from their investments (which result from the appreciation in value of the fund's portfolio companies). The ability to obtain lower rates was a powerful incentive to purchase equity instead of revenue participation rights because RPCs were taxed at higher ordinary income rates. If the present small differential between maximum ordinary income tax rates and capital gains tax rates continues, this incentive to purchase equity may become less important, making RPCs more common in venture financings. *See: Equity, Structure.*

Risk Capital is what venture capitalists provide to entrepreneurs. These investments of capital are risky because of the early stage of the companies, the lack of collateral to secure the investments, and their illiquid nature. This is why venture capitalists require annual rates of return in excess of 35 percent and a measure of control over company management. Most studies of venture capital investment reveal that as many as seven out of ten venture investments fail to meet their projections, thus justifying the rate of return venture firms require and the suspicion with which business plans are greeted by investors. *See: Pricing, ROI (Return on Investment), Venture Capital.*

ROI (Return on Investment) is the premium an investor receives for investing in a company when he liquidates his holdings. Venture capitalists expect high returns from their investments.

Venture investors express the return they want to make from an investment in terms of percentages, much the same way lenders price loans. By determining what compounded annual rate of return he wants from a given investment, a venture capitalist can then work with his projections for the company's growth to arrive at the percentage of the company's stock he needs to receive in order to do a funding.

What ROIs do most venture capitalists require to fund a company? They vary from company to company. The following chart give some general ranges, based on an economy supporting prime interest rates at or near 10 percent.

Company Stage	Compounded Annual ROI
Seed or start-up	40% and up
First and second stage	30% to 50%
Third stage and mezzanine	20% to 30%

How these rates of return translate into cost to a company depends in large part on how long it takes the investor to exit. The following table illustrates this fact.

Payoff	Compounded Annual ROI
Three times investment in three years	44%
Five times investment in three years	71%
Seven times investment in three years	91%
Four times investment in four years	41%
Three times investment in five years	25%
Five times investment in five years	38%
Seven times investment in five years	48%
Ten times investment in five years	58%

As these tables show, venture capital money is expensive. The longer management can delay its need for funding and the earlier it can provide an investor with an exit, the less expensive the money will be. *See: Pricing, Procrastination, Projections.*

S

Safe Harbors refer to exemptions from the registration requirements of federal and state securities laws that are so explicit in their requirements that they enable a company to offer and issue securities privately without fear of running afoul of the securities laws' registration requirements. The Reg D private placement exemptions and integration rules are examples of safe harbors. Whenever possible, companies should structure their offerings to fall within a safe harbor. By doing so, they reduce the risk that their offerings will be recharacterized as unregistered public offerings. Any such recharacterization could have disastrous effects upon the company's ability to raise money and could subject it and management to serious liabilities. *See: Integration, Private Placements, Reg D, 33 Act.*

SBA (Small Business Administration) refers to an agency of the U.S. government that lends money and guarantees loans to small companies. Because of funding cutbacks, however, the SBA's present activities are limited primarily to guaranteeing loans made to small companies by banks and other financial institutions.

These loan guarantees are administered under the SBA's "7(a) Loan Guarantee Program." Under the program, participating banks, business development corporations, and other institutional lenders evaluate potential borrowers, set the borrowing terms, and prepare the lending paperwork. They also set the interest rate (but are prohibited from charging more than 2.75 percent over prime). The SBA then guarantees up to 80 percent of qualifying loans, which decreases the lenders' risks and makes it more feasible for small companies to borrow.

The SBA relies extensively on its participating lenders to evaluate and service the guaranteed loans. Two of its programs demonstrate this reliance. Under the Certified Lenders Program, qualifying lenders are certified by the SBA and promised three-day turnaround on loan applications they submit to the SBA. "Preferred lenders" are actually delegated authority to extend SBA guarantees on loans that meet SBA guidelines.

Whichever type of SBA lender a company approaches, management should be prepared to meet numerous requirements. Each lender evaluates loan applications against its own and the SBA's requirements. Borrowers should expect questions relating to the company's capitalization, its ability to repay the loan, and the personal resources of its principals. To meet the SBA's requirements alone, management must show, among other things, that it owns a for-profit business that is not dominant in its industry (usually not too hard), and that it does not discriminate in employment practices.

The documentation for SBA guarantees is usually extensive, containing protective provisions that limit the manner in which the company can use the money loaned, require extensive personal guarantees from management, and require regular and extensive reporting to the lender. SBA-guaranteed loans are usually collateralized by "everything in sight," including the company's real property, receivables, inventory, equipment, stock, and even the personal assets of management.

The guarantee of a loan by the SBA makes money available to companies that might not otherwise be able to borrow at commercially reasonable rates. The SBA guarantee does not, however, reduce the lender's desire for company collateral or for the personal guarantees and property pledges of management. Nor does it reduce the requirements for covenants and restrictions in the loan documentation. This is because lenders still look to the borrowing company and its management as the parties primarily responsible for the loan. SBA lenders will foreclose against the assets of a company and its management. They will do everything within their power to avoid calling on the SBA guarantee, because in doing so they jeopardize their relationship with the SBA. *See: BDCs (Business Development Corporations), MESBICs (Minority Enterprise Small Business Companies), Promissory Notes, SBICs (Small Business Investment Companies), SBIR (Small Business Innovation Research).*

SBICs (Small Business Investment Companies) are

lending and investment firms that are licensed by the federal government. The licensing enables them to borrow from the federal government to supplement the private funds of their investors. Some of these funds engage only in making loans to small businesses or invest only in specific industries. The majority, however, are organized to make venture capital investments in a wide variety of businesses.

SBICs usually have at least $500,000 in private capital. Some have as much as $10 million. By using their special access to government loans, SBICs can leverage their private capital by as much as four to one. That is, if an SBIC invests $100,000 of its own money in a company, it can borrow another $300,000 from the federal government and invest that as well.

In practice, this means that SBICs almost always require that a large part of their investment in a company be in the form of loans or income-producing securities. This is because the majority of the funds they invest are borrowed moneys on which they have to pay interest and repay principal.

Other venture capital funds often require that part of their investment be in the form of a loan as well, but there is an important distinction between SBICs and other venture capital funds. SBICs, because they must immediately begin servicing the interest on their government loans, usually require a company to start making some payments to them on their investment earlier than a private venture capital fund will.

While this immediate debt service may change in the future, as a group SBICs presently tend to avoid the earliest stage investments when the risks are greatest. They do, however, represent a good source of funds for later stage companies whose prospects are more secure. If the prospects are secure enough, an SBIC will invest in a company that offers a more moderate potential for growth than might be required to attract a traditional or private venture capital firm. *See: CDCs (Community Development Corporations), MESBICs (Minority Enterprise Small Business Investment Companies), Venture Capitalists.*

SBIR (Small Business Innovation Research) refers to a U.S. government program that provides funding for research to businesses with 500 or fewer employees. In the right circumstances, the program can provide valuable seed capital for an entrepreneur's new product development activity.

The SBIR program was created by the Small Business Innovation Development Act of 1982. It requires major government agencies to allocate a portion of their research and development funds to small private businesses through the SBIR program.

The Small Business Administration (SBA) oversees the program and produces informational pieces which describe the program and the types of research for which funds are available. Each participating agency establishes its own funding and contract criteria. Participating agencies include the following:

- Department of Agriculture
- Department of Defense
- Department of Education
- Department of Energy
- Department of Health and Human Services
- Department of the Interior
- Department of Transportation
- Environmental Protection Agency
- National Aeronautics and Space Administration
- National Science Foundation
- Nuclear Regulatory Agency

The SBA periodically issues a listing of research and development projects for which each agency is soliciting proposals. A copy of the listing can be obtained by contacting the SBA. By responding to an agency's request for proposal (RFP), the entrepreneurial company can compete for the funds available to conduct the announced research. Some agencies will accept unsolicited research proposals.

Research grants are typically awarded in phases. The first phase consists of a grant of up to $50,000 to be used to evaluate the feasibility and scientific merit of the proposed research. If the first phase is completed successfully, the company can obtain up to $500,000 in the second grant phase to develop the subject technology over a one- or two-year period. Production contracts with the federal agency often follow successful completion of the second phase.

The newly developed technology is typically owned by the company subject to a limited use license to the funding agency. Solicitation and other procedures vary from agency to agency, so companies should investigate the agency's rules carefully before competing for its research funds. *See: SBA (Small Business Administration).*

S Corporations are a special kind of corporation identified in the Internal Revenue Code that are taxed differently from the more customary C corporations most people think of when they think of corporations.

S corporations differ from C corporations in one important particular: They are not taxed by the IRS as entities separate and distinct from their shareholders. In S corporations, the income and losses of the company pass directly to its shareholders. If the company earns $100,000 in profits during the year, its 50 percent shareholder would be responsible for showing 50 percent of the profit, or $50,000, on his tax return as income. If the company lost money during the year, each of its shareholders would be entitled to claim a portion of the company's losses on his individual tax return as a loss.

These profits and losses pass directly to the shareholders without regard to whether or how much money the company distributes to them. If the company makes a profit and needs it to fund operations, the shareholders will have to show that profit on their individual tax returns and pay taxes on it even though they receive no cash. Agreements can be made among shareholders and management to require cash payments that are sufficient to pay taxes.

In the past, when maximum individual tax rates exceeded corporate maximum tax rates, S corporations were used primarily during the early stages of company development while losses exceeded profits. With individual tax rates falling below corporate tax rates under 1986 tax reform, S corporations came to be used in many cases to actually reduce federal taxes paid on corporate earnings by effectively giving the company the benefits of its shareholders' lower maximum tax rates. Appropriate use of the S form will always depend, in part, on the relative tax rates of corporations and individuals. These rates are always subject to change.

The S form can reduce the cost to the shareholders of their investments in a company that is losing money by allocating back to those shareholders the company's losses in its first years. These losses can be used by the shareholders to reduce their income tax obligations and thereby effectively reduce their after-tax cost of investment. At the same time, however, the company loses the ability to use these losses to shelter future income from taxes and thereby increases the likelihood that it will need additional funding in the future.

S corporations are not particularly effective at attracting outside investors with the promise of allocating company losses to them to reduce their taxes. This is because losses and profits are allocated to S company shareholders on the basis of the number of shares held. In other words, an outside investor will only receive a portion of the company's losses equal to his percentage ownership. If he puts in $1 million and gets 40 percent of the stock, he will get only 40 percent of losses generated by the company's use of his money. If the company loses all of his $1 million, he will only get $400,000 of it.

Other devices, such as limited partnerships, permit more flexibility in the allocation of losses and profits and consequently are used more often than S corporations to attract investors who want to reduce the after-tax cost of their investments. Limited partnerships can be structured so that almost all of the company's losses are allocated to the outside investor. This means an investor who purchases a 40 percent interest in a limited partnership could, nonetheless, receive almost all of the losses attributable to the use of his $1 million even though he may only be entitled to receive 40 percent of the profits.

Establishing an S corporation requires strict compliance with a number of IRS requirements, including rules relating to the nature of the company's shareholders and its outstanding securities, and may not be available to all entrepreneurial companies. For example, S corporations are available only to companies organized under the laws of a state. Foreign corporations, even if they have assets or do business in the United States, cannot qualify. Even some domestic companies defined by the IRS as "ineligible corporations" (e.g., insurance companies, certain financial institutions, and other enumerated companies) cannot qualify. S corporations can have no more than thirty-five shareholders, all of whom must be individuals, estates, or certain qualifying trusts. And only one class of stock can be issued without jeopardizing the S corporation's tax status (although that class can be divided into subclasses with different voting rights). Certain consent and timing requirements must also be met to secure S corporation status.

As you might imagine, the flow-through of profits and losses is not without its complications. For one thing, losses can be used by a shareholder only to the extent of his "basis" in his stock. Initially, this basis equals the individual's purchase price for his stock plus his basis in any loans he makes to the company. As the company operates, this basis can fluctuate, however, generally increasing with company income and gains and decreasing with company losses. Also, losses generated to a shareholder may not be used to offset all types of income.

Because of the complexity of S corporations and the peculiarities of the manner in which they and their shareholders are taxed, entrepreneurs should always consult with their accountants and legal advisers before organizing S corporations. Failure to do so could result in unwanted surprises for the company and its shareholders. *See: Limited Partnerships, R & D Partnerships, Structure.*

SEC (Securities and Exchange Commission) is the

government agency that administers the 33 Act and other federal securities laws. It reviews public offering documents and promulgates rules and regulations interpreting the federal securities acts and establishing safe harbors from the registration requirements of the 33 Act. *See: Going Public, IPOs (Initial Public Offerings), Private Placements, Reg D, Restricted Securities, Safe Harbors, 10b5, 33 Act.*

Secrecy Agreements *See: Confidentiality Agreements.*

Seed Capital refers to financing obtained by a company

before it has completed developing a prototype of its product. Sometimes it refers to capital raised after a company has developed a prototype of its product but before it has manufactured any production units. This is the most difficult and expensive money to raise because it is needed before management can prove that the product will sell or that it can be produced and distributed at a competitive price. The entrepreneur's family, friends, relatives, and his personal savings are the primary sources of seed capital. *See: CDCs (Community Development Corporations), Stage Financing.*

Shareholders' Agreements are contracts entered into between company shareholders, usually at the insistence of a minority shareholder. A venture capitalist who does not acquire control with his purchase of company stock will usually require a shareholders' agreement as a condition of funding. Management that sells a controlling interest in its company's common stock normally insists upon a shareholders' agreement to ensure its continued ability to run the company.

Shareholders' agreements can take a variety of forms and can serve a variety of purposes. They are usually in writing and signed by persons who together own at least a majority of the outstanding shares of the company's voting stock.

Shareholders' agreements enable a minority shareholder to exercise more control over a company than he would have otherwise. (By voting his minority interest in the company's shares, he would have no control.) A venture capitalist, for example, will almost always insist that management agrees to vote its shares so that he will be ensured a seat on the company's board of directors. Sometimes an investor will ask for other types of control as well, such as the right to veto certain important financial decisions made by the directors.

Shareholders' agreements often contain other provisions affecting management and its relationship with its investors. These provisions commonly contain limitations on the manager's ability to sell his shares to outsiders and provide for the disposition of his shares in the event of his death or termination of employment. Shareholders' agreements are also commonly used for estate planning purposes.

Management should consider shareholders' agreements carefully. They should have a limited term and, in most cases, should terminate in the event of a public offering of the company's stock or sale of the company. *See: Benchmarks, Buy-Sell Agreements, Common Stock Control, Co-Sale Agreements, Cumulative Voting, First Refusal Rights.*

Shark Repellents are provisions in a company's charter and bylaws that make it more difficult for an outsider to gain operating control of a company. (The shark being repelled is the outsider who would change management if he gained control of the company.) Shark repellents are commonly used by managements of public companies in which outsiders have opportunities to acquire control by purchasing shares in the public market.

Common shark repellents include "super-majority" voting requirements (for example, 67 percent of shareholders) to approve a sale of the company, the staggered election of company directors, and the use of classes of voting stock, so that holders of publicly traded shares are entitled to elect only a minority of the board of directors. *See: Control, Going Public.*

Shopping refers to the practice of presenting a company's business plan to several investors simultaneously (a.k.a. "shopping the deal"). Yet many people advise companies against presenting their business proposals to several potential investors at the same time. It is bad form, they say, and makes venture capitalists think the companies are not serious about working with them.

The fact is, however, that few entrepreneurs have the time to let only one venture capitalist look at their investment proposal. Most venture capitalists take six to eight weeks to conduct their investigations and make investment decisions. At that rate, one or two rejections can cripple a promising company if it pursues only one investor at a time.

The better practice is to present the company's proposal to two to four carefully selected venture capitalists simultaneously, explaining to each that the company is doing this because it recognizes that most venture capital firms prefer to invest with other firms and that time pressures require the company to speak with a few select firms at the same time. Often, if an entrepreneur asks, investors will suggest other investors to whom the company can present its business plan.

Another good practice is to send an inquiry letter to a larger number of venture investors. The letter should identify the company, its business, the amount of money needed, and the way in which the money will be used. After providing this information, the letter can offer to send business plans to interested investors. Used in a mailing to venture firms that have invested in the company's industry and stage of investment before, this process can help management identify those investors who are currently funding companies like theirs. This, in turn, allows management to concentrate its efforts on investors who are interested and more likely to fund.

The following is the body of an inquiry letter that was sent to a number of investors around the country. The investors were selected based on their histories of funding companies in the company's industry. The letter generated significant interest and led to serious funding negotiations.

> Dear Investor:
>
> We are seeking first-stage investment capital for our business. Minimum investment requirements are $500,000 with a comprehensive package totaling $2.5 to 3 million. We have been in business for one year and can demonstrate rapid growth, achievement, and potential. All of our operating subsidiaries are involved with musical merchandise and high-tech electronic application to this field.
>
> We are interested in taking our companies public. Our management team is very experienced and already in place. I have enclosed an issue of *Musical Merchandise Review* (the trade publication) that features our company. This will provide you with some background information. We have made a significant impact on our industry with our merchandising ability as well as our rapid success.
>
> Please contact me personally if you are interested in learning more about our firm.
>
> Sincerely,

Entrepreneurs should be flexible in their search for funding and speak with lenders, individuals, family, friends, relatives, and other sources in addition to venture firms. A common mistake many entrepreneurs make when raising capital is limiting their searches to one type of investor. Many believe (mistakenly) that if they need capital, they must always get it from a venture capital fund.

Another common mistake is to assume that one investor will provide all of the debt and equity financing the company needs. In fact, most venture capital financings involve more than one investor. Many involve a separate lender who receives no equity for lending.

To improve the odds of being funded, management can separate its funding needs into debt and equity requirements and approach lenders and equity investors at the same time, asking each to commit to fund a portion of the company's total financing needs. Getting a commitment for part of a funding is often easier than getting one for all of it. This is particularly true when each investor's commitment is contingent upon the company securing the rest of the financing because each investor knows that his money will not be committed until another investor agrees enough with his positive assessment of the company to put his money down as well. Once a company gets its first commitment using this approach, other investors become easier to find and more inclined to join in. *See: Networking, Syndication, Venture Books, Venture Capitalists.*

Software Protection refers to the fact that both copyrights and trade secrets protection can be used to prevent others from misappropriating valuable company software. Often, this software is essential to the success of the company, and protecting it adequately is not only prudent but necessary to convince an outsider to invest his money in the company. Venture investors expect companies to take reasonable steps to protect their proprietary software and other valuable secrets from being misappropriated by their competitors.

Copyright and trade secrets protection each protects a different aspect of computer software, and both require the company to take certain actions to secure their protections. Copyrights protect the expression of ideas rather than the ideas themselves. That is, copyrights can prevent someone from using (copying) a program but not from using the ideas (algorithms) in the program to produce a new program that does the same thing.

Copyright protection is governed by federal statute and protects both published and unpublished works. To secure full copyright protection, a company must follow prescribed rules and file with the Federal Copyright Office within five years after the program is developed. Filings with the Copyright Office can be done in object code or source code, and there is a procedure that permits companies to file the first twenty-five and last twenty-five pages of a program printout. This procedure can help a company preserve its trade secrets in a program while obtaining copyright protection as well.

By contrast, trade secret protection protects ideas themselves rather than the expression of them. Trade secrets protection is governed by state law and protects only ideas that are kept secret. Protecting a trade secret through litigation involves proving that the trade secret exists, that it was disclosed only in confidence, and that the use or disclosure of the information complained about was obtained in violation of a confidence and to the injury of the company.

The existence of a trade secret is a matter of fact. The factors courts generally consider in determining whether a trade secret exists include the extent to which the information is known outside the company's business, the extent the information is known to employees and others involved in the business, the value of the information to the company and its competitors, the amount of money and effort expended to develop the information, and the ease or difficulty with which the information can be properly acquired by competitors. In other words, the more valuable the information and the more safeguards the company takes to protect that information, the easier it will be to prove a trade secrets case in court. Both trade secrets and copyright protection can provide a company with rights to money damages and to enjoin a competitor from using its misappropriated software.

The differences between copyright protection and trade secrets protection are not well understood by all software entrepreneurs. Some, particularly those whose software is a big-ticket item that is licensed to a relatively small number of licensees under contract, forgo copyright filings and rely solely on trade secrets protection to guard their rights in their programs.

This course of action can be dangerous, however, because it ignores some of the substantial advantages copyrights offer for protecting software. A better strategy is usually to claim the protection of both trade secrecy and the copyright laws. Securing both gives a company more ways to stop infringers from stealing its software and gives it access to the federal courts to pursue its claims. In many situations, copyright infringement cases are easier to prove in court than trade secret infringement cases, giving the company that obtains copyright protection a significant advantage over one that relies solely on trade secrecy.

A good practice when claiming copyrights or trade secrets protection is to mark the software medium (diskette) and program the software to display at sign-on a message identifying the rights claimed by the company. A sample notice claiming both protections follows:

©1993 by Software Company

All Worldwide Rights Reserved.

This work contains trade secrets of the Software Company. Any unauthorized use, copying, compiling, decompiling, or reverse engineering is strictly prohibited.

Care must be taken, however, whenever both copyright and trade secrecy protection are sought, to preserve the confidentiality of the software during the copyrighting process. The careless filing of materials with the copyright office or over-reliance on copyright protection in the wrong situation can lead to the loss of important trade secrecy rights in a computer program. A qualified attorney can advise management on the best strategy to follow to obtain the most protection available under both laws. *See: Copyrights, Trade Secrets.*

Specialty Funds are venture capital firms that invest their money only in companies or products that fall within an identified industry or field of endeavor. Utech Venture Capital Fund, headquartered in Baltimore and Atlanta, is one such focused fund. It invests "in ventures which offer a product or service directly, and not necessarily exclusively, related to the needs of the electric and gas utility industry." Other focused funds exist in other industries.

Specialty funds use their industry focus to help attract investors and give them an edge in identifying promising companies in their chosen industries. By specializing, they are able to develop industry-specific expertise that can not only help them understand and identify the potential of a new company in the industry, but that can also help them assist that company after they have made their investment.

Spending time to identify specialty funds in his company's industry can help an entrepreneur raise capital. Even funds that are not specialty funds tend to specialize in industries or stages of financings. Identifying the tendencies of investors can help a company focus its fund-raising activities and increase its chances for success. *See: Venture Capitalists for some sources containing listings of investors. See also: Corporate Venture Capital, Shopping, Value Added.*

Stage Financing refers to a method many investors use to reduce their risk when funding companies. Funding a company in "stages" means providing the money that has been committed in pieces as the company meets preestablished goals. Customarily, the company doles out the shares to the investor as the money is received. For example, an investor might agree to provide $800,000 to a company by paying $400,000 down, $200,000 when the company gets its first order, and $200,000 when it receives its first payment from an order. The stock sold to the investor might be issued in increments of five thousand shares up front, fifteen hundred shares when the first $200,000 payment is made, and one thousand shares when the last $200,000 is put in. (The earlier dollars buy more shares because there is more risk at the beginning.) Often, these goals are tied in some fashion to the financial projections contained in the company's business plan.

While the commitment is to fund the entire amount, the later stages of funding are contingent on the company attaining its goals. If the company fails, the investor is relieved of his obligation to fund any further. In this way, the investor can cut his losses when a company does not meet expectations. At the same time, the company gets a commitment for its full funding, which it can obtain by meeting its goals.

Stage financing also refers to the fact that most growing companies need funding at various points in their development. At each point, or stage, the company solicits new investors to fund the next phase of company growth.

Usually, a company goes through two or three venture "rounds" of financing before it is large and healthy enough to sell its stock on the public market. Each stage of financing can reduce management's percentage ownership in the company. As the company progresses, however, its stock should command a higher price in each successive stage. The reason for this is that the investor's risk decreases as the company succeeds and meets its goals. As a result, if management gave up 30 percent of its company's stock to attract $500,000 in venture capital the first time around, it may only cost an additional 15 percent of the company's stock to raise $1 million in the second round of financing.

The first stage of financing is commonly called "seed financing." This is money raised to make an idea for a product into a working prototype. Quite often, this money is invested by an individual or by the entrepreneur and his management team.

Seed money is the hardest to find, and the most expensive (in terms of equity). Because it is so expensive, many entrepreneurs try to forestall asking for equity investments from outsiders as long as possible. Investing his own savings is one way for an entrepreneur to delay or avoid this stage of financing. Borrowing against the equity in his house is another.

Start-up capital usually refers to money raised to modify a working or almost-working prototype product into a product that can be manufactured at a cost that allows the company to make a profit. It can be the first or second stage of a company's financing. Start-up capital is used to test-market products and prepare companies for their first round of product sales. This money is more readily available than seed capital.

Second- and third-tier financings come next (if they are needed). These are traditionally used to finance inventory and company expansions. If a second- or third-tier financing is used to fund a company expansion that enables the company to later conduct a public offering, it is referred to as a mezzanine financing.

In the dynamic world of venture capital and start-up companies, no two companies have the same capital needs or grow in the same way. If management delays the need to acquire seed money until its prototype is almost ready, one venture capitalist might consider the proposed investment a seed investment while another might consider it an early start-up financing. There is no magic to the labels. They are conventions that are casually observed in the industry to describe financings. *See: Benchmarks, Mezzanine Financing, Pricing, Procrastination, ROI (Return on Investment), Seed Capital, Start-Up Capital.*

Start-Up Capital refers to money raised to enable a company to get its working prototype product into production and to make initial marketing efforts. This money costs companies less equity per dollar of funding than seed capital does, but more than later-stage financings. *See: Mezzanine Financing, Seed Capital, Stage Financing.*

Stock Committee refers to a group of company officers and/or directors designated by a company's board of directors with the mandate of determining when and how additional shares of the company's stock should be issued to employees or others. Stock committees often allocate a pool of shares to employees as part of an incentive plan.

Venture capitalists will usually consent to the reservation of a small pool of shares to be issued to employees after closing of a funding even though the issuance of those shares will dilute the percentage interest of the investor. Often, however, the investor will want to participate in the allocation of these shares. One way for an investor to do this is to require that they be issued by a stock committee of which he is a member. *See: Board Committees, ISOs (Incentive Stock Options).*

Strategic Partnerships. *See: Joint Ventures.*

Structure refers to the combination of debt and equity an investor receives for funding a company. Sometimes called "deal structure," it covers the timing of his funding and the protections and exits he receives. For example, one structure may call for $500,000 to be invested in a company in return for 20 percent of the company's outstanding stock. The deal might require all of the money to be invested at once and might include piggyback registration rights and a right of first refusal. Another structure might call for the money to be invested in stages as the company meets certain benchmarks and might require preferred stock or convertible debentures to be issued to the investor. That investor might also receive demand and piggyback registration rights, rights of first refusal, puts, and options to purchase additional shares. Both might require antidilution rights, but the amount of antidilution protection they require may be very different.

Most of the negotiations in a venture financing revolve around the price and structure of the proposed deal. Revising a structure can turn a bad deal into a good one, or vice versa. To negotiate effectively, management and its advisers must understand the ramifications of the various deal structuring devices employed by investors and the concerns of investors those devices are designed to address. Those devices and concerns are addressed elsewhere in this book. *See: Antidilution Provisions, Benchmarks, Buy-Sell Agreements, Convertible Securities, Co-Sale Agreements, Debentures, Earnouts, Earnups, Equity Penalties, Exits,*

First Refusal Rights, LBO (Leveraged Buyout), Leverage, Liquidity Agreements, Negotiation, Personal Guarantees, Pricing, Projections. Puts, Registration Rights, Revenue Participations, Shareholders' Agreements, Stage Financing, Take-Away Provisions, Weighted Average Antidilution.

Subordinated Debt is borrowed money that stands to be repaid after other debts but before company shareholders receive consideration in the event the company is liquidated. Subordinated debt is frequently used in venture financings to provide investors with a way to increase their return on investment or to withdraw a portion of it as debt repayment without unduly prejudicing the company's ability to obtain other borrowings.

Since it stands behind other debt if the company liquidates, subordinated debt is often treated as equity by other lenders. That is, lenders are willing to extend additional credit to the company as if the debt did not exist, as long as their debt matures and is repaid before the subordinated debt. This usually means that the subordinated debt agreement not only contains specific language subordinating it to other debt but that its maturity date occurs after that of the company's other debt. Therefore, the later the payback on subordinated debt, the easier it is for a company to borrow additional funds.

Subordinated debt provides a company with cash, usually with a long-term payback, and gives the investor a way to withdraw a portion of his investment without adverse tax consequences. Sometimes subordinated debt contains a convertibility feature that allows the investor to convert it into shares of stock. This gives the investor the flexibility to withdraw his funds as debt repayment or to convert to share ownership if the company's stock is selling for a good price. *See: Cash Flow, Convertible Securities, Debentures, Structure.*

Summary refers to a synopsis of the key points of a business plan. Sometimes referred to as an executive summary, it appears at the beginning of a business plan and highlights certain aspects of the company's proposal that are particularly important to prospective investors. It is one of the most important parts of a business plan.

The importance of the summary can be illustrated by a simple fact: Few venture capitalists will spend more than five or ten minutes on a business plan before deciding whether they are interested enough to study it seriously. The two portions of the business plan most venture capitalists focus on during this critical first reading are the summary and the financial information (projections). If the summary does not heighten their interest, few investors will turn to the financials or consider the company further.

Because of its importance in getting investors to investigate further, the summary should be prepared with particular care. It should be short (two to four pages is ideal), concise, descriptive, well organized, and enticing.

A lot to ask of a summary? Maybe, but while no professional investor is likely to invest in a company on the basis of two pages of reading, many will decide against investing just that quickly. To ensure that the potential investor does not discard the company's business plan after reading only the summary, the plan writer should be sure it provides the investor with the right information about the company.

An effective summary should include the following information:

- *Company identity and contact.* Give the name, address, and telephone number of the company. The name of the person the investor should contact and how he or she may be reached should be prominently displayed.

- *Business of the company.* A short description of the company's business should be given here. How did it get started? What is its market niche, and why will it succeed?

- *Management.* What are the strengths of the company's key management personnel? A short itemization of the relevant accomplishments of key management members should be given.

- *The product.* This paragraph should contain a short description of the company's product and what makes it unique. A brief analysis of the company's competition and why management believes its product will succeed in the marketplace should also be included.

- *Funds required.* How much money does the company need? Does management have any preference as to equity versus debt? If the funds are requested on a staged basis, this should also be set forth. If there is collateral available, it should be described.

- *Use of funds.* How the company plans to use the funds should be detailed here.

- *Financial history.* A short financial history of the company should be provided here. This can be done in a narrative or in a chart listing four or five key figures such as revenues, income or loss, assets, liabilities, and net worth for each year of the company's operation.

- *Projections.* This section should contain a summary of the key elements of the company's projections for the next three to five years.
- *Exits.* Any plans the company has to go public or to provide the investor with other exits in the next three to five years should be spelled out. The investor wants to know how he will get his money out.

See: Business Plan, Business Plan Format, Negotiation, Three Questions.

Sweat Equity is the hard work, long hours, worry, and fatigue that a founding entrepreneur suffers to make his company succeed. The stock initially issued to the entrepreneur usually costs a great deal less than stock later sold to investors who take less risk. This difference between the higher price paid for shares of the company's stock by investors and the price paid by the company's founders is the value of sweat equity. *See: Bargain Stock.*

Syndications are venture investments that are shared among several investors, with each providing part of the total funding to the company. Syndications are popular among venture investors because they allow them to spread their money over more deals and diversify their risks. They also allow them to share information with other investors.

Sometimes an investor who is willing to invest part of the money is not willing to put together the syndicate necessary to provide the rest. Such an investor is less attractive to a company than one who is willing to help find all the capital a company needs. A good question to ask any interested venture capitalist is whether he is able to provide all the funding needed by the company. If not, ask if he will syndicate the investment. Most established funds will do so.

A problem that sometimes accompanies a syndicated funding is the desire of each investor to have a seat on the company's board of directors. As a rule, management should try to limit its outside investor group to the same number of board seats management would have given one investor had he provided all of the funding. Usually, this means one or two board seats for the investor group with the investors choosing among themselves who will represent them on the board. Others may attend board meetings and consult with management, but only the ones serving on the board will be entitled to vote.

This encourages the syndication's members to cooperate among themselves so that management is not distracted by disagreements among its investors. At the same time, it preserves a small working board of directors and gives management the ability to tap into the expertise and contacts of each investor. *See: Lead Investor, Shopping, Underwriters.*

T

Tag-Along Provisions are agreements that require one or more parties, usually company management, to include another party, usually an outside investor, in future opportunities they receive to sell their stock. They are also referred to as co-sale agreements. *See: Co-Sale Agreements.*

Take Away Provisions are agreements between an investor and management that entitle the investor to penalize management when the company does not achieve agreed-upon results. The penalty is often the reduction in management's shareholdings or in its ability to operate the company independently. Take away provisions are most prevalent in financings where the company sells a controlling interest to the investors and management contracts with the investor to maintain operating control so long as company results are acceptable. They are also common in earnups, leveraged buyouts (LBOs) and other transactions where management's participation is predicated upon its achieving certain results. See: *Earnouts, Earnups, LBO (Leveraged Buyout), Management Agreements, Operating Covenants, Shareholders' Agreements, Structure, Voting Trusts.*

Technology Development Centers are facilities designed to help entrepreneurs create viable businesses from their innovations. Many state governments and universities sponsor programs to promote the development of new high-tech companies in their areas. These programs locate several services in one facility, sometimes called technology development centers or technology incubators. If one exists nearby, management may be well advised to explore the services the center can provide.

Some centers provide "incubator assistance" by giving entrepreneurs inexpensive space, access to university research facilities, and consulting services on a reduced-fee basis. Others assist in company promotion and in obtaining government permits and licenses. If the program is an established one, it also may provide assistance in obtaining funding. *See: Incubators.*

10b5 refers to a provision in the federal securities laws that prohibits fraudulent and misleading activities in securities transactions. State securities acts contain similar prohibitions. All of these provisions prescribe severe penalties for violators. As a result, the use of fraudulent or misleading material, the making of misstatements, or the existence of material omissions in a securities offering can have serious consequences to a company and its management.

The text of the 10b5 provision reads as follows:

It shall be unlawful for any person, directly or indirectly, by the use of any means or instrumentality of interstate commerce, or of the mails, or of any facility of any national securities exchange,

1. to employ any device, scheme, or artifice to defraud,

2. to make any untrue statement of a material fact or omit to state a material fact necessary in order to make the statements made, in the light of the circumstances under which they were made, not misleading, or

3. to engage in any act, practice, or course of business which operates or would operate as fraud or deceit upon any person,

in connection with the purchase or sale of any security.

The combined effect of 10b5 and similar state laws is to make it very risky, and potentially costly, to deal in company securities in a way that is not honest, straightforward, and in strict compliance with the law.

The securities laws, rules, and regulations are complex, and courts have been expansive in their interpretations of the 10b5 and other antifraud provisions of the securities laws. To avoid problems, legal counsel should always be consulted before securities are offered for sale. *See: Going Public, Lawyers, Private Placements, Reg D, SEC (Securities and Exchange Commission), 33 Act.*

Think Capital is a company's technology and the brainpower of key employees who supply the company with its technological edge. In high-tech companies, the protections taken to preserve this think capital are very important to prospective investors. These protections include careful documentation of the company's title to important technologies, safeguards to prevent the theft or loss of company secrets, agreements to prevent competition by employees, and incentives to keep key personnel employed with the company. *See: Confidentiality Agreements, Copyrights, Golden Handcuffs, Noncompete Agreements, Patents, Software Protection, Trade Secrets.*

33 Act refers to the federal Securities Act of 1933. Any time a company attempts to raise capital through the issuance of securities, it becomes subject to a variety of laws regulating the offering and selling of securities. The most important of these are the 33 Act and the states' securities acts. These laws make it unlawful for any person to offer, sell, or deliver any "security" unless a registration statement meeting requirements contained in the law is in effect as to the security or an exemption to the registration requirements applies.

The securities these laws apply to have been broadly defined by the statutes and courts. They include corporate stock and debt instruments as well as similar interests issued by individuals, partnerships, and joint ventures. They also include other types of "investment contracts" that are not commonly thought of as securities.

Detailed disclosure or ready access to information must be given to investors in connection with a securities offering. This is generally true whether the offering is registered or exempt from registration. This disclosure is usually made through the use of a prospectus (also referred to as an offering circular) that contains pertinent information concerning the offering, the securities being offered, and the entity issuing the securities. In limited circumstances, however, such as venture capital transactions involving only certain specially qualified (or "accredited") investors, the information may be made available in other ways that do not involve the preparation of an extensive offering memorandum. *See: Going Public, Investment Reps, IPOs (Initial Public Offerings), Private Placements, Reg D, Restricted Securities, SEC (Securities and Exchange Commission), 10b5.*

Three Questions investors invariably ask: How much money do you need? How will you spend it? How will I get it back? To obtain funding, entrepreneurs must be prepared to answer these questions intelligently. *See: Business Plan, Due Diligence, Exits, Summary.*

Track Record is a person's or company's operating history. The best and most relevant track record management can have is to have created a successful business before. Second best is experience working in the company's industry or in other start-ups. The better the track record management has, the easier it will be to attract capital to the company, and to attract it at a favorable price.

Track records can transcend a company or industry in special cases. For example, John Sculley's track record with PepsiCo enabled him to establish himself at Apple Computer. In this case, Sculley's track record in a specific functional area was so outstanding that it could transcend an industry. *See: Entrepreneur, Five Factors, Turnarounds.*

Trademarks are words or design elements that identify companies' products and distinguish them from others. Service marks identify and distinguish services. Businesses can prevent others from using their marks on competitive products by following federal and state laws that govern trademarks and service marks.

Trademarks can become very important to new companies as they build their reputations for their products. In general, they must be registered, used in commerce, and identified as a trademark or service mark in order for companies to protect them.

Companies can conduct searches to be sure a mark is available before they begin using it so that they can avoid promoting a mark they cannot protect or use. The first type of search that can be conducted is one of the records of the trademark office to determine whether anyone has already registered the mark. If no registration is found, the company can next pay a service bureau to conduct a common-law search to see if the mark is already being used in commerce in an unregistered form. If the mark clears both searches, the chances are good that it can be registered and protected. Company counsel can advise on the best and most appropriate method for conducting these searches. *See: Copyrights, Patents, Trade Secrets.*

Trade Secrets are all of a company's proprietary know-how that gives it an advantage in the marketplace. Different states define trade secrets differently, but most state laws only protect trade secrets that are not generally known to competitors and only when the company takes actions to identify and protect them.

Unlike patents, which entitle the holder to preclude others from using patented technologies, trade secrets protection prevents others from using company technologies only by keeping them secret. If others discover the company's secrets by "reverse engineering" or by developing the same secrets on their own, they cannot be stopped from using the knowledge. Trade secrets protection can prevent others from stealing company secrets, but only if the company takes appropriate actions to prevent unauthorized disclosure of its information.

Confidentiality and secrecy agreements with company employees, owners, and consultants who have access to secrets are common methods of protecting trade secrets. Investors who put money into companies with valuable secrets usually require the companies to enter into secrecy agreements with their employees. Some also require management members to enter into secrecy and noncompete agreements directly with the investors.

Confidentiality agreements alone will not protect company secrets. Other measures must be taken to ensure the secrecy of the information. These include limiting access to company secrets (only those persons who need to know the secrets to perform their jobs and who are bound by a secrecy agreement should have access), marking secrets as confidential, and distinguishing between secrets and nonsecrets. Material containing company secrets should be stored in a safe place and destroyed when it is no longer needed so that it cannot be "leaked."

Trade secrecy laws vary from state to state. Some states, for instance, distinguish between technical trade secrets and nontechnical confidential information, allowing a company to protect nontechnical information only by contract and only for a limited period of time. Some states require stricter definitions of technical trade secrets than they do of nontechnical confidential information. Others make no distinction at all. All prescribe definite limits to the availability of trade secrecy protection.

Attempts to extend protection beyond these legal limits, even if inadvertent, can jeopardize the trade secrecy protection a company relies upon. This, coupled with the fact that companies must comply with all of the conditions and requirements set out by their states' laws before they can claim trade secrecy protection, makes it important for companies to have an experienced professional review the precautions they take to protect their secrets and to review the form of any secrecy agreements they use. *See: Confidentiality Agreements, Lawyers, Software Protection, Think Capital.*

Turnarounds are situations in which new funds are needed to get a company out of trouble. Some turnarounds involve companies whose management buys out the controlling shareholders and tries to turn around the company and make it profitable. Certain managers excel at turn-around situations because they have the necessary skills and guts to make the hard decisions required in these cases. These managers are called turnaround specialists. Their track records are far more important than the industry or the companies they corrected. One of the most famous turnarounds in recent history was Lee Iacocca's revitalizing of Chrysler Corporation. *See: LBO (Leveraged Buyout).*

U

Underwriters refer to stock brokerage firms and others who market and sell company securities to the public.

Most public securities offerings are sold (or underwritten) by underwriters who specialize in such transactions. The sale is typically conducted through a syndicate of firms that are selected by the company's underwriter. The managing underwriter in the syndicate (the one selected by the company) attempts to select the right combination of underwriters to achieve a distribution of the company's shares among private individuals and institutional purchasers that will ensure a good price in the offering and adequate trading in the shares after it is completed. The managing underwriter usually continues to support the company in the financial community after the offering by making a market in the company's stock, providing research and analysis on the company for investors, organizing communications with investors and potential investors, and generally helping the company create a following in the investment community.

Because of the variety of services they provide, and because their ability to provide those services efficiently can affect not only the offering price of the company's shares but also their continuing strength in the public marketplace, the selection of the right underwriter is important. Among the characteristics management should consider when selecting an underwriter are the following:

- *Stature within the financial community.* The underwriter's professional reputation as an investment banker can determine, in large part, his ability to put together a strong syndicate to sell the company's shares. The strength of the syndicate can, in turn, influence the quality of the investors attracted to the offering.

- *Experience in the company's industry.* Underwriters develop reputations within industries. An underwriter who is experienced at taking businesses public in the company's industry can enhance the credibility of the company's offering. Experience can also help an underwriter price a company's shares properly so that the company's shares hold their price or increase in price after the offering is sold.

- *Research reputation.* The company's managing underwriter will be a primary source of information about the company to the financial community. It is helpful, therefore, to select an underwriter whose analysts are experienced and follow the company's industry closely. An underwriter's reputation for reliable research in a company's industry can help sustain investor interest in the company's stock.

- *Ability to support the market.* Once issued, the company's stock will be traded on the over-the-counter market. The ability of the underwriter as a "market-maker" to support the market is important. By purchasing and selling the company's stock in the market, the "market-maker" gives the company's stock needed liquidity, which helps stabilize trading prices.

It is a good practice to interview several underwriters before selecting one to conduct a public offering. Accountants, bankers, lawyers, and other entrepreneurs can make introductions to underwriters. A good deal of information about underwriters and the types of deals they do also can be obtained by watching the financial press, particularly the *Wall Street Journal*. Underwriters regularly run advertisements (called "tombstones" by the trade) that show public offerings they have done and the syndicate members who participated. *See: Going Public, Investment Bankers, IPOs (Initial Public Offerings), Syndications.*

Unit Offerings are sales of company securities when more than one type of security is sold as a single unit, or when investors are required to purchase securities in blocks of shares. The term is frequently used to refer to private placements or public offerings where investors are offered the opportunity to purchase "units" that consist of a share of stock and a warrant to purchase more stock in the future. *See: Going Public, IPOs (Initial Public Offerings), Penny Stock, Private Placements.*

Unlocking Provisions are mechanisms that enable investors to disengage their financial arrangements with management. One typical unlocking provision is a buy-sell agreement, which allows an investor to force management either to buy the investor's shares at a price he sets or sell its own shares to the investor for the same price. Another provision creates a mechanism through which either management or the investor can force the other to sell its interest in the company to a third party or buy the stock of the other party. Typically, this arrangement allows either management or the investor to accept a third party's offer to buy the company's assets or the stock of both management and the investor. The other party must then either buy the first party's shares at the per-share price contained in the third-party offer or sell his interest, along with the interests of the other shareholder, to the third party. *See: Buy-Sell Agreements, Exits, Liquidity Agreements.*

Upside is the potential profit an investor hopes to receive from his investment under ideal circumstances. It is what the venture capitalist measures against the downside when evaluating a company. The greater the upside and the more likely it will be obtained, the less the investor will require in return for his investment.

When businessmen speak of "dollar signs dancing in their eyes," they are envisioning the upside. For venture investors, the upside represents the potential for their shares to appreciate significantly. This can be achieved by company growth and success and can be supplemented by the market increasing the stock's price-earnings (P/E) ratio. *See: Downside, P/E, Price-Earnings Ratio, Pricing, ROI (Return on Investment).*

V

Value Added refers to the knowledge, management advice, and related nonmonetary input investors sometimes offer a young company. Many venture investors do provide more than money to their portfolio companies. They provide management with the benefit of their experience with emerging growth companies. They also help management by using their contacts in the company's industry and with other financial sources.

This value added by the venture capitalist can be important but is difficult to measure. In addition to the risk (or downside), it is the reason many professional venture firms try to charge a management fee to the portfolio company. Entrepreneurs often fail to see the "value added" of a venture capitalist's advice at first, but many recognize it later when the value of the advice becomes more apparent. *See: Consulting Agreements, Geography, Management Agreements.*

Venture Books cover many issues of interest to entrepreneurs. Several of them deal with venture capital financing and are worth reviewing. One of the best is *Pratt's Guide to Venture Capital Sources*, edited by Stanley E. Pratt and Jane K. Harris and published by Venture Economics, Inc. It comes in two volumes and contains a series of articles on venture capital financing. It also contains a detailed listing of venture capital firms, the sizes of their funds, the types of companies they invest in, and the names and telephone numbers of their principals. The price is approximately $100. A less expensive, one-volume version of the book without the venture capital firms listing is also available under the title *How to Raise Venture Capital*.

Other good books include the following:

- *Venture Capital Handbook* by David Gladstone (Reston Publishing Co., 1984). This guide for entrepreneurs is written by a practicing venture capitalist.

- *High Tech Start Up —The Complete How-To Handbook for Creating Successful New High Tech Companies* by John L. Nesheim (Electronic Trend Publications, 1992). The author of this helpful book is president of Saratoga Venture Finance and a long-time Silicon Valley financial officer.

- *How to Start, Finance, and Manage Your Own Small Business* by Joseph R. Mancuso (Prentice-Hall, Inc., 1978). This volume has a good section describing the manner in which venture capitalists analyze business plans. Also by Joseph Mancuso is *How to Write a Winning Business Plan*.

- *Venture Capital Investing* by David Gladstone (Prentice-Hall, Inc., 1988). This book for would-be investors discusses the venture capitalist's approach to investing in private companies.

- *The Handbook for Raising Capital: Financial Alternatives for Emerging and Growing Businesses* edited by Lawrence Chimerine, Robert F. Cushman, and Howard Ross (Dow-Jones Irwin, 1986). This is a collection of articles by investment bankers, accountants, lawyers, and others about methods of raising money.

See: Business Plan, NASBIC (National Association of Small Business Investment Companies), National Venture Capital Association, Venture Capitalists.

Venture Capital is money invested in a company or individual at high risk to the investor, usually in situations in which the company is unable to secure needed funds from traditional lending sources, such as a commercial loan from a bank. Usually, the status of the company is such that the investor will be unable to withdraw his money in the near future. Venture capital can be invested through the purchase of stock (equity), by making a loan (debt), or through a combination of the two. Often, venture capital investments come bundled with management assistance and oversight by the investor, known as value added services.

Venture capital investors require a very high rate of return and thus only invest in companies with good prospects for rapid growth. Companies most likely to obtain venture capital are those that promise to appreciate quickly and which envision a public offering or company sale in five years or less. Turnarounds and leveraged buyouts (LBOs) are also good prospects for venture capital investors. *See: Adventure Capitalists, Angels, BDCs (Business Development Corporations), CDCs (Community Development Corporations), Corporate Venture Capital, Emerging Growth Companies, LBO (Leveraged Buyout), P/E, Pools, Pricing, ROI (Return on Investment), SBICs (Small Business Investment Companies), Specialty Funds, Turnarounds, Value Added, Vulture Capitalists.*

Venture Capital Clubs are informal groups of venture capitalists, entrepreneurs, financial strategists, accountants, and lawyers that meet regularly to discuss matters of interest, exchange ideas, and share opportunities. They provide a common meeting ground for persons interested in entrepreneurial activity. There are many of these clubs across the United States. If one exists nearby, management should explore the opportunities it provides to become acquainted with the venture capital infrastructure of the area. *See: Networking, Venture Capital Conferences.*

Venture Capital Conferences are forums at which venture capitalists meet to exchange information and hear presentations from companies seeking funding. Typically, the sponsor of the conference screens applicants who want to present their companies' funding needs. The applicants who pass the screening then describe their opportunities in short oral presentations to an audience of investors. Interested investors can follow up with the entrepreneurs later in the conference.

The best sources of information about upcoming venture capital conferences are local accounting or law firms, which may cosponsor them, local venture firms, which may participate as plan screeners, and local colleges and universities with entrepreneurship courses, which may provide facilities or professors as speakers. *See: Networking, Shopping.*

Mistakes I Made at a Business Plan Forum

The opportunity to present my entrepreneurial business idea to the New Ventures Workshop at the Harvard Business School was too great to pass up. I thought of the exposure to a roomful of investors eager to pour hundreds of thousands of dollars into my venture and the tremendous profits their dollars would initiate. I thought of the feedback I would get from the panelists — surely they would be impressed with the idea, and with me as an entrepreneur. No doubt they would be equally impressed with my wife (the company's cofounder) and her ability to handle the public relations aspects of the firm. Certainly people would be thrusting Offers To Purchase at me before the presentation was over. I made a note to have Offers To Purchase with me.

Judging by the process of getting scheduled, how bad could the experience be? Mr. Burt Alimansky, Chairman of the Workshop, was patient and thorough as he explained the ground rules of the workshop and the costs involved. I would need to submit my complete business plan to the panelists at least ten days before, and have handouts ready for the audience. To be most effective, he recommended that I accompany my talk with a slide show, highlighting certain key aspects of the business. He provided me with a suggested outline and asked for my suggestions for panelists. For $350, I would benefit from the candid business advice of four panelists, all of whom would be familiar with the industry in which I hope to operate. And one of the panelists would be a venture capitalist — so if the deal looked good, I'd make contact right there.

I began working on the presentation months in advance. For a public talk, I thought I would omit a lot of the routine financial information, and instead include more industry background. Instead of pie charts and pro formas, I decided to include color slides depicting the problems the industry is having, and how the new company expects to solve them. Instead of iffy sales projections, I listed the product benefits and hinted at possible unit sales. I wrote jokes into the script here and there to provide comic relief.

Wrong, wrong, wrong. The first comment from the first panelist was, "Mr. Cohen, when it comes to investments of this magnitude, you shouldn't be joking." The first comment from the second panelist was, "Mr. Cohen, instead of providing sales projections, you've given us conjecture. We need solid sales projections, for every product, for ten years, in order to properly analyze your chances for success."

The third panelist said, "Mr. Cohen, your slides are very nice, but you haven't shown us a single slide of your product, nor have you provided a Sources and Uses Statement. As investors, how will we know where our money is going?" And the fourth panelist said, "Mr. Cohen, you've wasted your time and ours. Without detailed financials, including projected profit and loss statements and balance sheets for each of the first ten years, the industry background you've provided is nothing but interesting reading. You've got a lot of work to do."

And so, $350 and many late nights working on the plan later, I learned to heed the advice I had been hearing from venture capitalists for many years: Don't go looking for capital until the plan is complete, and answers the questions investors are bound to ask. The Plan Forums ... aren't places for theatrics or creativity. Just stick to the basics, and make sure all your homework is done. Don't agree to be a presenter unless you are certain your plan is complete, including all financials and the shareholder's agreement. Because, like the Emperor and his new clothes, if you're naked up there, somebody will notice.

From an editorial by Steven M. Cohen,
which appeared in the September 1985 issue
of Venture's Capital Club Monthly

Venture Capitalists are those professional money managers who provide risk capital to businesses. Venture capitalists come in many forms and specialize in different ways, but all share the common trait of making investments in privately held companies that have the potential to provide them a very high rate of return on their investments.

Venture capitalists include over one thousand private funds, fewer than 100 companies funded by public offerings of their securities, bank and corporate subsidiaries charged with investing budgeted funds, and private individuals, often called "adventure capitalists" or "angels." Venture firms can be highly leveraged companies, such as SBICs and MESBICs, or completely unleveraged.

Some good sources for identifying venture capitalists interested in a given industry are

- The National Association of Small Business Investment Companies (NASBIC), 1199 N. Fairfax Street, Suite 200, Alexandria, VA 22314; (703) 683-1601
- The National Venture Capital Association, 1655 North Fort Myer Drive, Arlington, VA 22209; (703) 351-5267.
- *The Corporate Finance Sourcebook* (National Register Publishing Company, annual editions).
- *Pratt's Guide to Venture Capital Sources* (Venture Economics, Inc., annual editions).

See: Adventure Capitalists, Angels, BDCs (Business Development Corporations), CDCs (Community Development Corporations), Corporate Venture Capital, MESBICs (Minority Enterprise Small Business Investment Companies), Pools, SBICs (Small Business Investment Companies), Specialty Funds, Venture Books, Vulture Capitalists.

Vesting Schedules refer to a method used to make a person's stock ownership contingent upon some future event, such as the passage of time or the achievement of a stated goal. They are commonly a part of an agreement pursuant to which management or certain company employees are denied full ownership rights in their shares until the future.

When a vesting schedule applies, an employee is granted the rights to a specified number of shares of the company's stock, but those shares do not really become his until certain defined events have occurred. For example, an employee may be granted ten thousand shares of the company's common stock "subject to vesting." Those shares may vest upon his remaining employed with the company for five years. Each year, for instance, two thousand of his shares may vest and become his providing he is still employed by the company. If he remains with the company for the full five years, he will receive all ten thousand shares. If he leaves after three years of employment, he will receive certificates for only six thousand shares.

Vesting schedules often tie an employee's rights to own shares to employment longevity and some other factor such as company earnings or sales. Often, they are used with noncompete agreements and employment incentives to encourage effort and loyalty from important employees.

Because of the complexity of the Internal Revenue Code and certain technicalities it contains, anyone who receives stock subject to vesting requirements should consult with an attorney or accountant to determine the tax effect of receiving it and the advisability of filing an 83(b) election. *See: 83(b) Elections, Golden Handcuffs.*

Voting Agreements are also referred to as shareholders' agreements. These are contracts, usually in writing, that are signed by two or more shareholders and govern the manner in which those shareholders will vote their shares of company stock. In most situations, if shareholders holding a majority of the shares of voting stock agree to vote their shares together, they can control a company. Voting agreements are commonly used by minority shareholders to ensure themselves a seat on a company's board of directors or to restrict the issuance of additional shares of a company's stock. *See: Control, Shareholders' Agreements.*

Voting Trusts are agreements used to transfer control from management to an investor if the company does not meet its goals. They work by placing management's stock in a trust with the investor's shares. The trustee is instructed to vote the entrusted shares as the investor directs if the company fails to meet its goals. Voting trusts are the exception, not the rule, these days. *See: Benchmarks, Control, Take Away Provisions, Voting Agreements.*

Vulture Capitalists is a term used by disappointed entrepreneurs to describe investors who refused their deals or who they believe demanded too much equity in return for funding. The term is sometimes used by an entrepreneur to identify an investor who has exercised a contractual right and taken an action the entrepreneur disagrees with, such as firing management or liquidating the company. The term is pejorative and reflects the attitude of a disgruntled entrepreneur.

Venture capitalists do not invest in companies to make friends. They invest to make money. Without profits, the investors in the venture capitalist's fund or pool will not participate in later funds, and the venture capitalist will go out of business. As a result, venture capitalists are extremely picky about the companies they invest in and how well they perform. They do not want their portfolio companies to fail. They can be expected to exercise any contractual rights they have to prevent a portfolio company from failing, even if doing so makes them a vulture capitalist in the eyes of the entrepreneur. *See: Deal Flow, Golden Rule, Venture Capitalists.*

W

Warrants are a form of stock option that entitles an investor to purchase shares of company stock in the future at a price fixed by the warrant. Warrants are commonly given in connection with a loan or equity investment in a company. The holder is given the warrant as an inducement. He can "exercise the warrant" by paying cash for the share price on the warrant or, if given with a loan, by canceling a portion of the debt equal to the warrant exercise price. When they are issued in connection with a loan, warrants are often called equity kickers to refer to their ability to give debt investors an opportunity to share in the company's capital appreciation. *See: Options.*

We Always Do It This Way is a phrase management sometimes hears from an investor or his lawyer, normally, at the point where management has negotiated the main deal points with the investor and the parties are in the process of putting that deal onto paper. Suddenly, the investor's lawyer presents the company with forty-five pages of representations and warranties he wants management to sign. Management remembers the investor saying that he wanted to keep the deal simple, with the minimum reps and warranties. Management protests, and the lawyer says, "But we always do it this way."

Management is supposed to roll over and gladly comply with the lawyer's request. After all, they always do it that way. This is the first venture capital financing the company has been involved in, and the investor has done dozens. So he must know what's appropriate. Right?

Wrong. There are certain conventions observed in venture capital financings, including "normal" types of representations and warranties that companies and their managements customarily make. Nonetheless, management is entitled to receive a rational explanation about anything the venture capitalist asks it to do that it does not understand (or agree with).

An explanation such as "we always do it this way" is not enough. That explanation probably means the company has been presented with the lawyer's standard form, which he always uses as a starting point in negotiations. Like all standard forms, much of what is in it will not apply to the company or its funding.

"We always do it this way" implies that the way the investor did his deals in the past is the way the current deal should be done. But this company and its needs are different from all those other deals. And, while it may be unrealistic to expect an investor to abandon the deal structure or basic deal documents that have worked well for him, it is realistic to expect him to deal openly with management and to explain why each provision of his documents is necessary. *See: Boilerplate, Reps and Warranties.*

Weighted Average Antidilution refers to a form of antidilution protection that is commonly used by venture capital investors to prevent the value of their shareholdings from being unfairly reduced by later share sales at lower prices. The weighted average method uses a formula to determine the dilutive effect of a later sale of cheaper securities and grants the investor enough extra shares for free to offset that dilutive effect.

A common weighted average formula multiplies the number of shares of company stock outstanding, including the protected venture investor's shares, by the price per share paid by the venture investor for his shares, adds to that product the amount of the new investment (number of new shares times per share price), and divides the sum by the total number of shares outstanding after the new investment. The result of this calculation gives a new price per share for the protected venture investor that is then divided into the dollar amount he invested to determine the total number of shares he should have. The difference between this number and the number of shares the venture investor already owns is the number of new shares the venture becomes entitled to receive for free.

The weighted average antidilution method is usually more favorable to management shareholders than the ratchet method described earlier. Under that method, the protected investor is entitled to get enough free shares to reduce his price per share to the same price paid by the later investor regardless of the number of shares sold to the later investor. (See: Ratchets.) The following example illustrates how great the difference can be between the operation of a ratchet and a weighted average antidilution provision.

Assume that an investor buys 300,000 shares of company stock for $2 per share when management owns 700,000 shares. A later investor buys 200,000 shares from the company for $1 per share. A ratchet would give the first investor 300,000 new shares for free in order to reduce his average price per share to $1.

The weighted average method issues far fewer new shares to the protected investor. Under that method, the first investor's 300,000 shares are added to management's 700,000 shares and then multiplied by $2. The $2 million product of this calculation is then added to the $200,000 paid by the second investor giving a sum of $2.2 million. This amount is divided by the total number of shares outstanding after the second sale, 1,200,000, to give the new average price for the first investor. That price is $1.83 per share. When divided into the $600,000 invested by the first investor this yields 327,869 total shares to which the first investor is entitled, requiring the company to issue him 27,869 free shares.

The chart below compares how the two antidilution methods fared in the example. The difference in results from the two methods would be even more dramatic if fewer shares were sold to the second investor.

Comparison of Antidilution Methods

	Weighted Average	*Ratchet*
Shares bought by investor	300,000	300,000
Free shares to investor	27,869	300,000
Total investor shares	327,869	600,000
Total outstanding shares	1,227,869	1,500,000
Average investor share price	$1.83	$1.00
Percent owned by investor	26.6	40.0
Percent owned by management	57.0	46.6
Percent owned by second investor	16.4	13.4

See: Antidilution Provisions, Dilution (Percentage), Ratchets.

We Never Exercise Our Rights Under This Section

is a phrase that often follows "We always do it this way" and begins with "Don't worry...." It is designed to comfort management when the venture investor insists on a particularly onerous provision. Sometimes the phrase is different: "We don't expect to have to use this provision" or "We never use this provision, but we always require it."

Management should be careful when someone asks for something they insist they will never use. If they really will not use it then they do not need it. *See: Boilerplate, Reps and Warranties, We Always Do It This Way.*

Windows is a phrase used in two distinctly different contexts, but in both cases the aspect of timing is crucial.

Firstly, venture capitalists are very sensitive to the timing of the introduction of a company's new product into the market. If the technology is too revolutionary, the cost of creating a market for the product may be prohibitive. On the other hand, if the product does not have enough to distinguish it from its competition, it may be too late for the product to gain a profitable market share. That period of time when the company's technology is new enough to distinguish its products in the marketplace but not too new so that no one understands its application is sometimes called "the window of opportunity." Introducing the product "while the window is open" is critical to a company's prospects for success.

Secondly, window is used to refer to the period of time when the stock market is receptive to new issues of stock in the particular industry of a company. When one company conducts a successful initial public offering in computer software, for example, other software companies will rush to complete their offerings "while the window is open." *See: Five Factors, Going Public, IPOs (Initial Public Offerings), Market Research.*

Z

Zeal is something investors want and expect to see in entrepreneurs they fund. No one wants to invest in a lethargic entrepreneur. *See: Commitment, Entrepreneur.*

SUBJECT INDEX

IV. Growth Company Valuation